UkrainianLessons.com

Anna Ohoiko

Ukrainian Phrasebook for Helping Refugees

Essential phrases for communication with Ukrainians
More than 1500 practical words and phrases
Transliteration to Latin characters
Free audio online

Ukrainian Lessons
2022

Cover design: Oleksandra Siryk (Олександра Сірик)
Book interior design: Oleksandra Siryk (Олександра Сірик)
Production editor: Anna Ohoiko (Анна Огойко)
Copy editors: Kateryna Smuk (Катерина Смук), Kiana Smith
Assistant: Maryna Serbyna (Марина Сербина)

Abstract:
Since the beginning of the brutal Russian invasion of Ukraine in 2022, people around the world #StandWithUkraine and put enormous effort into supporting the refugees. This phrasebook is for everyone helping Ukrainian people — at the borders, at immigration centers, at humanitarian organizations, in their homes, or at a distance. It includes 20 practical chapters of the most important Ukrainian words and phrases to facilitate communication and demonstrate care. Additional links to expand certain topics make this book an excellent basis for further Ukrainian learning.

Publisher Contact Information
Anna Ohoiko
anna@ukrainianlessons.com

Paperback ISBN: 978-91-986937-2-0
Ebook ISBN: 978-91-986937-3-7

Table of Contents

Introduction

Welcome! **Ласкаво просимо!** Laskávo prósymo!

This is the first phrase you could say to Ukrainians when you meet them at the borders, immigration centers, humanitarian organizations, or at your home. Even if you do not pronounce it perfectly yet, and even if it is the only phrase you know, **it will make a difference**. It will show your care, hospitality, and support of Ukraine.

This phrasebook is packed with words and expressions like that. It will not provide you with everything you need to start speaking in Ukrainian right away. However, it will equip you with the **essentials**, give you **ideas of what to say or ask** and hopefully inspire you to **continue learning the language**.

Here are some things to consider before you start using the phrasebook.

1. This book consists of **20 chapters/topics** that you should familiarize yourself with on the previous page. Once you know which topics are included, you will be able to quickly find one when you are in a particular situation and need to communicate with Ukrainians.

2. Usually, I try not to use Latinized Ukrainian in my teaching because it does not reflect correct pronunciation. This time speed of communication is more important than quality. That is why I included **transliterations** of all words and phrases on the right side of the charts.

   Please keep in mind that this is a **transliteration and not** a phonetic transcription. It means it is not always the exact way to pronounce the word, it is just the Ukrainian alphabet in Latin characters.

   I used the official Ukrainian governmental guidelines of transliteration to Latin characters. The only exception is the first *Alphabet* chapter — it has a phonetic transcription of all letters.

3. You can access my **audio recordings** of all the words and phrases if you follow the links or QR codes at the beginning of each chapter. These are useful if you have some time to practice before you actually communicate with Ukrainians.

   A good exercise would be to try and read the phrase in Ukrainian out loud, then listen and check with my audio, then repeat with corrections. You can also record yourself and compare the result with my voice.

4. In most of the chapters, the **formal forms** of Ukrainian were used (**ви, ваш**). These forms are used when talking to people you do not know or who are not your close friends or family of the same age.

   In chapter 8, *Giving Support,* I provided both formal and informal forms so that you could support your close friend as well as people you do not know well. In chapter 17, *Children*, there are only **informal forms (ти, твоя)** as we use them with kids.

5. Among the lists of expressions, you will find boxes with some **grammar info** or useful **links to free resources** that will help you expand certain topics.

If you have any **feedback**, tips, or suggestions for phrases to include in the second edition of the book, feel free to email me at anna@ukrainianlessons.com.

Glory to Ukraine! **Слава Україні!** Sláva Ukraíni!

Anna Ohoiko
Founder of UkrainianLessons.com

1. Alphabet

 Link to audio: ukrainianlessons.com/ph-alphabet

А а	[a]	like **a** in st**a**rt		**Н н**	[en]	like **n** in **n**o
Б б	[be]	like **b** in **b**est		**О о**	[o]	like **o** in p**o**rt
В в	[ve]	like **v** in **v**an		**П п**	[pe]	like **p** in **p**ark
Г г*	[he]	close to **h** in **h**ike		**Р р**	[er]	close to **r** in **r**ug
Ґ ґ	[ge]	like **g** in **g**o		**С с**	[es]	like **s** in **s**top
Д д	[de]	like **d** in **d**og		**Т т**	[te]	like **t** in s**t**op
Е е	[e]	like **e** in t**e**st		**У у**	[u]	like **oo** in p**oo**l
Є є	[je]	like **ye** in **ye**t		**Ф ф**	[ef]	like **f** in **f**at
Ж ж	[zhe]	like **s** in vi**s**ion		**Х х**	[kha]	like **wh** in **wh**o
З з	[ze]	like **z** in **z**oo		**Ц ц**	[tse]	like **ts** in lo**ts**
и	[y (i)]	close to **i** in d**i**d		**Ч ч**	[che]	like **ch** in **ch**ess
І і	[i]	like **ee** in m**ee**t		**Ш ш**	[sha]	like **sh** in **sh**ort
Ї ї	[ji]	like **yie** in **yie**ld		**Щ щ**	[shcha]	like **shch** in fre**sh ch**erries
Й й	[jot]	like **y** in **y**es		**ь**	[mjakyj znak]	makes the previous consonant soft
К к	[ka]	like **k** in **k**ey		**Ю ю**	[ju]	like **you** in **you**
Л л	[el]	like **l** in **l**emon		**Я я**	[ja]	like **ya** in **ya**rd
М м	[em]	like **m** in **m**om				

Learn how to **pronounce each letter in detail** with more examples at:
ukrainianlessons.com/alphabet

2. Essential Words & Phrases

 Link to audio: **ukrainianlessons.com/ph-essential**

Hello!	Добрий день!	Dóbryi den!
Hi! (informal)	Привіт!	Pryvít!
Good morning!	Доброго ранку!	Dóbroho ránku!
Good evening!	Добрий вечір!	Dóbryi véchir!
Yes	Так	Tak
No	Ні	Ni
Excuse me; Sorry	Вибачте	Výbachte
Please	Будь ласка	Bud láska
Thanks!	Дякую!	Diákuiu!
Thank you very much!	Дуже дякую!	Dúzhe diákuiu!
You are welcome.	Будь ласка.	Bud láska.
My name is...	Мене звати...	Mené zváty...
What is your name?	Як вас звати?	Yak vas zváty?
Nice to meet you!	Дуже приємно!	Dúzhe pryiémno!
Likewise! (nice to meet you)	Взаємно!	Vzaiémno!
Please come in.	Заходьте, будь ласка.	Zakhódte, bud láska.
Please sit down.	Сідайте, будь ласка.	Sidáite, bud láska.
I don't know.	Я не знаю.	Ya ne znáiu.
Of course.	Звичайно.	Zvycháino.
No problem.	Без проблем.	Bez problém.
Have a good trip!	Щасливої дороги!	Shchaslývoi doróhy!
Take care.	Бережіть себе.	Berezhít sebé.
All the best.	На все добре.	Na vse dóbre.
Goodbye!	До побачення!	Do pobáchennia!

question words	питальні слова	pytálni slová
Who?	**Хто?**	Khto?
Who are you by nationality?	Хто ви за національністю?	Khto vy za natsionálnistiu?
What?	**Що?**	Shcho?
What are you doing?	Що ви робите?	Shcho vy róbyte?
What? (used with a noun)	**Який? Яка? Яке? Які?**	Yakýi? Yaká? Yaké? Yakí?
What is your address?	Яка ваша адреса?	Yaká vásha adrésa?
Whose?	**Чий? Чия? Чиє? Чиї?**	Chyi? Chyiá? Chyié? Chyí?
Whose children are these?	Чиї це діти?	Chyí tse díty?
Where?	**Де?**	De?
Where did you work?	Де ви працювали?	De vy pratsiuvály?
Where to?	**Куди?**	Kudý?
Where are you heading to?	Куди ви прямуєте?	Kudý vy priamúiete?
Where from?	**Звідки?**	Zvídky?
Where did you come from?	Звідки ви приїхали?	Zvídky vy pryíkhaly?
When?	**Коли?**	Kolý?
When did you cross the border?	Коли ви перетнули кордон?	Kolý vy peretnúly kordón?
How?	**Як?**	Yak?
How are you?	Як ви?	Yak vy?
Why?	**Чому?**	Chomú?
Why did you decide that?	Чому ви так вирішили?	Chomú vy tak výrishyly?

How many? **How much?**	**Скільки?**	Skílky?
How old are you? (= How many years do you have?)	**Скільки вам років?**	Skílky vam rókiv?
Which? (by order)	**Котрий? Котра? Котре? Котрі?**	Kotrýi? Kotrá? Kotré? Kotrí?
What time is it? (= Which hour is it?)	**Котра година?**	Kotrá hodýna?

> Practice your **question intonation** in the Ukrainian Lessons Podcast's episode #35:
> ukrainianlessons.com/episode35

pronouns	**займенники**	zaiménnyky
I	**я**	ya
you (singular informal)	**ти**	ty
he	**він**	vin
she	**вона**	voná
it	**воно**	vonó
we	**ми**	my
you (formal or plural)	**ви**	vy
they	**вони**	voný
my	**мій**	mii
your (singular informal)	**твій**	tvii
his	**його**	yohó
her	**її**	yií
its	**його**	yohó
our	**наш**	nash
your (formal or plural)	**ваш**	vash
their	**їхній**	yíkhnii

> Learn Ukrainian **pronouns with a song** in the Ukrainian Lessons Podcast's episode #2:
> ukrainianlessons.com/episode2
>
> Practice Ukrainian **possessive pronouns with family members** in the episode #7:
> ukrainianlessons.com/episode7

family	сім'я	simiá
wife	дружина	druzhýna
husband	чоловік	cholovík
child	дитина	dytýna
children	діти	díty
daughter	дочка	dochká
son	син	syn
mother	мати	máty
father	батько	bátko
grandmother	бабуся	babúsia
grandfather	дідусь	didús
sister	сестра	sestrá
brother	брат	brat
cousin (female)	двоюрідна сестра	dvoiúridna sestrá
cousin (male)	двоюрідний брат	dvoiúridnyi brat
aunt	тітка	títka
uncle	дядько	diádko

days of the week	дні тижня	dni týzhnia
Monday	понеділок	ponedílok
Tuesday	вівторок	vivtórok
Wednesday	середа	seredá
Thursday	четвер	chetvér
Friday	п'ятниця	piátnytsia
Saturday	субота	subóta
Sunday	неділя	nedília

You can also learn **days of the week and months** in the episode #15
of Ukrainian Lessons Podcast:
ukrainianlessons.com/episode15

time	час	chas
today	сьогодні	sohódni
tomorrow	завтра	závtra
day after tomorrow	післязавтра	pisliazávtra
yesterday	вчора	vchóra
day before yesterday	позавчора	pozavchóra
day	день	den
night	ніч	nich
morning	ранок	ránok
evening	вечір	véchir
hour	година	hodýna
minute	хвилина	khvylýna
second	секунда	sekúnda
week	тиждень	týzhden
month	місяць	mísiats
year	рік	rik
next week	наступного тижня	nastúpnoho týzhnia
last week	минулого тижня	mynúloho týzhnia
next month	наступного місяця	nastúpnoho mísiatsia
last month	минулого місяця	mynúloho mísiatsia
next year	наступного року	nastúpnoho róku
last year	минулого року	mynúloho róku

months	місяці	misiatsí
January	січень	síchen
February	лютий	liútyi
March	березень	bérezen
April	квітень	kvíten
May	травень	tráven
June	червень	chérven
July	липень	lýpen
August	серпень	sérpen
September	вересень	véresen
October	жовтень	zhóvten
November	листопад	lystopád
December	грудень	hrúden

colors	кольори	kolorý
black	чорний	chórnyi
blue (dark)	синій	sýnii
blue (light)	блакитний	blakýtnyi
brown	коричневий	korýchnevyi
green	зелений	zelényi
grey	сірий	síryi
orange	помаранчевий	pomaránchevyi
pink	рожевий	rozhévyi
purple	фіолетовий	fiolétovyi
red	червоний	chervónyi
white	білий	bílyi
yellow	жовтий	zhóvtyi

Watch this video to practice **colors with fun exercises**:
ukrainianlessons.com/video-colors

useful adjectives	**корисні прикметники**	korýsni prykmétnyky
big	великий	velýkyi
small	малий	malýi
cheap	дешевий	deshévyi
expensive	дорогий	dorohýi
light	легкий	lehkýi
heavy	важкий	vazhkýi
old	старий	starýi
young	молодий	molodýi
new	новий	novýi
clean	чистий	chýstyi
dirty	брудний	brudnýi
hot	гарячий	hariáchyi
warm	теплий	téplyi
cold	холодний	kholódnyi
beautiful	гарний	hárnyi
safe	безпечний	bezpéchnyi
dangerous	небезпечний	nebezpéchnyi
fast	швидкий	shvydkýi
slow	повільний	povílnyi
easy	простий	prostýi
difficult	складний	skladnýi

In Ukrainian, adjectives change their endings according to the nouns that follow them.
For example: **гá́рний** хлопець, **гá́рна** дівчина, **гá́рне** кошеня, **гá́рні** діти

To learn more about using adjectives in Ukrainian, watch this short video lesson:
ukrainianlessons.com/video-adjectives

useful adverbs	корисні прислівники	korýsni pryslívnyky
always	завжди	závzhdý
often	часто	chásto
sometimes	інколи	ínkoly
rarely	рідко	rídko
never	ніколи	nikóly
left	ліворуч	livóruch
right	праворуч	pravóruch
near	близько	blýzko
far	далеко	daléko

You can easily form adverbs out of adjectives. For example:
деше́вий (adjective) – **де́шево** (adverb), **дороги́й** (adjective) – **до́рого** (adverb).
You can see more examples on this page:
ukrainianlessons.com/adjectives-and-adverbs

useful verbs	корисні дієслова	korýsni diieslová
be	**бути**	búty
I am	я (є)*	ya (ie)
you are	ти (є)*	ty (ie)
he / she is	він / вона (є)*	vin / voná (ie)
we are	ми (є)*	my (ie)
you are	ви (є)*	vy (ie)
they are	вони (є)*	voný (ie)

*є is almost always omitted in present tense

do, make	**робити**	robýty
I do	я роблю	ya robliú
you do	ти робиш	ty róbysh
he / she does	він / вона робить	vin / voná róbyt
we do	ми робимо	my róbymo
you do	ви робите	vy róbyte
they do	вони роблять	voný róbliat

eat	їсти	yísty
I eat	я їм	ya yim
you eat	ти їси	ty yisý
he / she eats	він / вона їсть	vin / voná yist
we eat	ми їмо	my yimó
you eat	ви їсте	vy yisté
they eat	вони їдять	voný yidiát

give	давати	daváty
I give	я даю	ya daiú
you give	ти даєш	ty daiésh
he / she gives	він / вона дає	vin / voná daié
we give	ми даємо	my daiemó
you give	ви даєте	vy daieté
they give	вони дають	voný daiút

go (on foot)	іти	itý
I go	я іду	ya idú
you go	ти ідеш	ty idésh
he / she goes	він / вона іде	vin / voná idé
we go	ми ідемо	my idemó
you go	ви ідете	vy ideté
they go	вони ідуть	voný idút

go (by transport)	їхати	yíkhaty
I go	я їду	ya yídu
you go	ти їдеш	ty yídesh
he / she goes	він / вона їде	vin / voná yíde
we go	ми їдемо	my yídemo
you go	ви їдете	vy yídete
they go	вони їдуть	voný yídut

have	мати	máty
I have	я маю	ya máiu
you have	ти маєш	ty máiesh
he /she has	він / вона має	vin / voná máie
we have	ми маємо	my máiemo
you have	ви маєте	vy máiete
they have	вони мають	voný máiut
know	знати	znáty
I know	я знаю	ya znáiu
you know	ти знаєш	ty znáiesh
he / she knows	він / вона знає	vin / voná znáie
we know	ми знаємо	my znáiemo
you know	ви знаєте	vy znáiete
they know	вони знають	voný znáiut
like	подобатись	podóbatys
I like	мені подобається	mení podóbaietsia
you like	тобі подобається	tobí podóbaietsia
he / she likes	йому / їй подобається	yomú/yii podóbaietsia
we like	нам подобається	nam podóbaietsia
you like	вам подобається	vam podóbaietsia
they like	їм подобається	yim podóbaietsia
look	дивитись	dyvýtys
I look	я дивлюсь	ya dyvliús
you look	ти дивишся	ty dývyshsia
he / she looks	він / вона дивиться	vin / voná dývytsia
we look	ми дивимось	my dývymos
you look	ви дивитесь	vy dývytes
they look	вони дивляться	voný dývliatsia

say	**казати**	kazáty
I say	я кажу	ya kazhú
you say	ти кажеш	ty kázhesh
he / she says	він / вона каже	vin / voná kázhe
we say	ми кажемо	my kázhemo
you say	ви кажете	vy kázhete
they say	вони кажуть	voný kázhut
see	**бачити**	báchyty
I see	я бачу	ya báchu
you see	ти бачиш	ty báchysh
he / she sees	він / вона бачить	vin / voná báchyt
we see	ми бачимо	my báchymo
you see	ви бачите	vy báchyte
they see	вони бачать	voný báchat
take	**брати**	bráty
I take	я беру	ya berú
you take	ти береш	ty berésh
he / she takes	він / вона бере	vin / voná beré
we take	ми беремо	my beremó
you take	ви берете	vy bereté
they take	вони беруть	voný berút
talk	**говорити**	hovorýty
I talk	я говорю	ya hovoriú
you talk	ти говориш	ty hovórysh
he / she talks	він / вона говорить	vin / vona hovóryt
we talk	ми говоримо	my hovórymo
you talk	ви говорите	vy hovóryte
they talk	вони говорять	vony hovóriat

think	**думати**	dúmaty
I think	я думаю	ya dúmaiu
you think	ти думаєш	ty dúmaiesh
he / she thinks	він / вона думає	vin / voná dúmaie
we think	ми думаємо	my dúmaiemo
you think	ви думаєте	vy dúmaiete
they think	вони думають	voný dúmaiut

understand	**розуміти**	rozumíty
I think	я розумію	ya rozumíiu
you think	ти розумієш	ty rozumíiesh
he / she thinks	він / вона розуміє	vin / voná rozumíie
we think	ми розуміємо	my rozumíiemo
you think	ви розумієте	vy rozumíiete
they think	вони розуміють	voný rozumíiut

want	**хотіти**	khotíty
I want	я хочу	ya khóchu
you want	ти хочеш	ty khóchesh
he / she wants	він / вона хоче	vin / voná khóche
we want	ми хочемо	my khóchemo
you want	ви хочете	vy khóchete
they want	вони хочуть	voný khóchut

If you would like to learn more about **how verbs work in Ukrainian**,
check out these resources:
Grammar Point: Verb conjugations in Ukrainian — ukrainianlessons.com/fmu57
Basics of Past Tense — ukrainianlessons.com/episode26
Basics of Future Tense — ukrainianlessons.com/episode28
First Verb Conjugation — ukrainianlessons.com/episode22
Second Verb Conjugation — ukrainianlessons.com/episode24
Verbs of Motion — ukrainianlessons.com/motion
Reflexive verbs — ukrainianlessons.com/reflexive-verbs
Imperative Mood — ukrainianlessons.com/episode111
Imperfective vs Perfective Verb Aspect — ukrainianlessons.com/episode91

3. Basic Needs

 Link to audio: **ukrainianlessons.com/ph-needs**

to need	потрібно / треба	potríbno / tréba
I need	Мені потрібно / треба	Mení potríbno / tréba
You need (singular informal)	Тобі потрібно / треба	Tobí potríbno / tréba
He needs	Йому потрібно / треба	Yomú potríbno / tréba
She needs	Їй потрібно / треба	Yii potríbno / tréba
We need	Нам потрібно / треба	Nam potríbno / tréba
You need (formal or plural)	Вам потрібно / треба	Vam potríbno / tréba
They need	Їм потрібно / треба	Yim potríbno / tréba

Do you need anything?	Вам щось потрібно?	Vam shchos potríbno?
What do you need?	Що вам потрібно?	Shcho vam potríbno?
It is free of charge.	Це безкоштовно.	Tse bezkoshtóvno.
How can I help you?	Як я можу вам допомогти?	Yak ya mózhu vam dopomohtý?
How can we help?	Як ми можемо допомогти?	Yak my mózhemo dopomohtý?
How do you feel?	Як ви почуваєтесь?	Yak vy pochuváietes?
Aren't you cold?	Вам не холодно?	Vam ne khólodno?
Do you have any pain?	У вас щось болить?	U vas shchos bolýt?

Do you want...?	Ви хочете...?	Vy khóchete...?
to eat	їсти	yísty
to drink	пити	pýty
to wash yourself	помитися	pomýtysia
to wash your hands	помити руки	pomýty rúky
to sleep	спати	spáty

... is here	... тут	... tut
... is there	... там	... tam
toilet	туалет	tualèt
shower	душ	dush
bathroom	ванна	vánna
kitchen	кухня	kúkhnia
your bed	ваше ліжко	váshe lízhko
your room	ваша кімната	vásha kimnáta
your documents	ваші документи	váshi dokuménty
food	їжа	yízha
water	вода	vodá
fridge	холодильник	kholodýlnyk
toiletries	засоби гігієни	zásoby hihiiény

Here you can...	Тут ви можете...	Tut vy mózhete...
take a shower	прийняти душ	pryiniáty dush
take a bath	прийняти ванну	pryiniáty vánnu
sleep	спати	spáty
eat	їсти	yísty
take food	брати їжу	bráty yízhu
make tea or coffee	приготувати чай чи каву	pryhotuváty chai chy kávu
cook	готувати	hotuváty
pray	молитися	molýtysia

Do you need ...?	**Вам треба...?**	Vam tréba...?
Do you have...?	**У вас є...?**	U vas ye...?
Here is/are...	**Ось...**	Os...
water	вода	vodá
food	їжа	yízha
soap	мило	mýlo
toothpaste	зубна паста	zubná pásta
toothbrush	зубна щітка	zubná shchítka
towel	рушник	rushnýk
clothes	одяг	ódiah
sanitary pads	прокладки	prokládky
tampons	тампони	tampóny
diapers	підгузки	pidhúzky
phone	телефон	telefón
sim card	сім-карта	sim-kárta
charger	зарядка	zariádka
blanket	ковдра	kóvdra
toys	іграшки	íhrashky
money	гроші	hróshi
housing	житло	zhytló
psychological help	психологічна допомога	psykholohíchna dopomóha
legal assistance	юридична допомога	yurydýchna dopomóha

4. Help

 Link to audio: ukrainianlessons.com/ph-help

help	**допомога**	dopomóha
to help	допомагати	dopomaháty
Help!	Допоможіть!	Dopomozhít!
We need help here.	Тут потрібна допомога.	Tut potríbna dopomóha.
What happened?	Що сталось?	Shcho stálos?
Can I help you?	Вам потрібна допомога?	Vam potríbna dopomóha?
May I help you?	Я можу вам допомогти?	Ya mózhu vam dopomohtý?
How can I help you?	Як я можу вам допомогти?	Yak ya mózhu vam dopomohtý?
I want to help you.	Я хочу вам допомогти.	Ya khóchu vam dopomohtý.
Please wait here.	Будь ласка, зачекайте тут.	Bud láska, zachekáite tut.
I will come back.	Я повернусь.	Ya povernús.
You can trust me.	Ви можете мені довіряти.	Vy mózhete mení doviriáty.
Don't worry.	Не хвилюйтесь.	Ne khvyliúites.
I will wait here with you.	Я почекаю тут з вами.	Ya pochekáiu tut z vámy.
I am getting somebody who can help.	Я знайду когось, хто зможе допомогти.	Ya znaidú kohós, khto zmózhe dopomohtý.
Somebody will come and help you.	Хтось прийде і допоможе вам.	Khtos pryidé i dopomózhe vam.

5. Legal Procedures & Documents

 Link to audio: ukrainianlessons.com/ph-legal

your first name	ваше ім'я	váshe imiá
your last name	ваше прізвище	váshe prízvyshche
your address	ваша адреса	vásha adrésa
gender	стать	stat
male	чоловік	cholovík
female	жінка	zhínka
adult (male / female)	дорослий / доросла	doróslyi / dorósla
child	дитина	dytýna
date of birth	дата народження	dáta naródzhennia
date of move	дата переїзду	dáta pereízdu
occupation	вид діяльності	vyd diiálnosti
place of birth	місце народження	místse naródzhennia
country of destination	країна призначення	kraína pryznáchennia
country of transit	країна транзиту	kraína tranzýtu

> Listen to a common conversation about **asking where someone is from**
> in the podcast episode:
> Talking about where you live and where you come from — ukrainianlessons.com/episode4

marital status	сімейний стан	siméinyi stan
married (male / female)	одружений / заміжня	odrúzhenyi / zamízhnia
single (male / female)	неодружений / незаміжня	neodrúzhenyi / nezamízhnia
divorced (male / female)	розлучений / розлучена	rozlúchenyi / rozlúchena
widower / widow	вдівець / вдова	vdivéts / vdová

| nationality | національність | natsionálnist |
| citizenship | громадянство | hromadiánstvo |

Ukrainian (male / female)	українець / українка	ukraínets / ukraínka
citizen of Ukraine (male / female)	громадянин / громадянка України	hromadiányn / hromadiánka Ukraíny
foreigner (male / female)	іноземець / іноземка	inozémets / inozémka
refugee (male / female)	біженець / біженка	bízhenets / bízhenka

Learn more about **how to talk about nationalities in Ukrainian** in the podcast episode:
How to introduce yourself in Ukrainian — **ukrainianlessons.com/episode3**

documents	документи	dokuménty
passport	паспорт	pásport
internal passport (ID card)	внутрішній паспорт (ID картка)	vnútrishnii pásport (ID kártka)
international passport	закордонний паспорт	zakordónnyi pásport
animal passport	паспорт тварини	pásport tvarýny
stamp from the border	штамп з кордону	shtamp z kordónu
driver's license	посвідчення водія	posvídchennia vodiiá
birth certificate	свідоцтво про народження	svidótstvo pro naródzhennia
visa	віза	víza
photo	фотографія	fotohráfiia
translation	переклад	peréklad
insurance	страхування	strakhuvánnia
application	заява	zaiáva
registration	реєстрація	reiestrátsiia
form	форма	fórma
temporary immigration permit	дозвіл на тимчасову імміграцію	dózvil na tymchasóvu immihrátsiiu

You need to...	Вам треба...	Vam tréba...
register	зареєструватись	zareiestruvátys
fill out a form	заповнити форму	zapóvnyty fórmu
submit an application	подати заявку	podáty zaiávku
Do you want to be registered as a refugee?	Ви хочете зареєструватися як біженець?	Vy khóchete zareiestruvátysia yak bízhenets?
Do you know what help you are entitled to?	Ви знаєте, на яку допомогу ви маєте право?	Vy znáiete, na yakú dopomóhu vy máiete právo?
Why are you afraid to return to your country?	Чому ви боїтесь повертатися у свою країну?	Chomú vy boités povertátysia u svoiú kraínu?
appointment times	години прийому	hodýny pryiómu

You have the right of...	У вас є право на...	U vas ye právo na...
asylum	притулок	prytúlok
appeal	оскарження	oskárzhennia
family unity	єдність родини	yédnist rodýny
financial support	фінансову підтримку	finánsovu pidtrýmku
free movement	вільне пересування	vílne peresuvánnia
healthcare	охорону здоров'я	okhorónu zdoróvia
residence	місце проживання	místse prozhyvánnia

6. Using Numbers

 Link to audio: ukrainianlessons.com/ph-numbers

number	число	chysló
numbers	числа	chýsla
zero	нуль	nul
one	один	odýn
two	два	dva
three	три	try
four	чотири	chotýry
five	п'ять	piat
six	шість	shist
seven	сім	sim
eight	вісім	vísim
nine	дев'ять	déviat
ten	десять	désiat
11	одинадцять	odynádtsiat
12	дванадцять	dvanádtsiat
13	тринадцять	trynádtsiat
14	чотирнадцять	chotyrnádtsiat
15	п'ятнадцять	piatnádtsiat
16	шістнадцять	shistnádtsiat
17	сімнадцять	simnádtsiat
18	вісімнадцять	visimnádtsiat
19	дев'ятнадцять	deviatnádtsiat
20	двадцять	dvádtsiat
21	двадцять один	dvádtsiat odýn
22	двадцять два	dvádtsiat dva

30	тридцять	trýdtsiat
40	сорок	sórok
50	п'ятдесят	piatdesiát
60	шістдесят	shistdesiát
70	сімдесят	simdesiát
80	вісімдесят	visimdesiát
90	дев'яносто	devianósto
100	сто	sto
200	двісті	dvísti
300	триста	trýsta
400	чотириста	chotýrysta
500	п'ятсот	piatsót
600	шістсот	shistsót
700	сімсот	simsót
800	вісімсот	visimsót
900	дев'ятсот	deviatsót
thousand	тисяча	týsiacha
two thousand	дві тисячі	dvi týsiachi
three thousand	три тисячі	try týsiachi
four thousand	чотири тисячі	chotýry týsiachi
five thousand	п'ять тисяч	piat týsiach
six thousand	шість тисяч	shist týsiach
million	мільйон	milión
billion	мільярд	miliárd

> Practice your **Ukrainian numbers** as well as that tricky **И pronunciation**
> with this podcast episode:
> Numbers in Ukrainian + Pronunciation Trainer — <u>ukrainianlessons.com/episode5</u>

How old are you?	**Скільки вам років?**	Skílky vam rókiv?
I am 36 years old.	**Мені 36 років.**	Mení 36 rókiv.
one year	один рік	odýn rik
two / three / four years	два / три / чотири роки	dva / try / chotýry róky
five / six … years	п'ять / шість … років	piat / shist … rókiv

In this chapter, you will notice that we use different forms of nouns depending on the final numeral of the number. There can be **three different forms**:

1

один рік, двадцять один рік, сто один рік etc.

2, 3, 4

два роки, три роки, чотири роки, сорок три роки etc.

other

п'ять років, шість років, сім років, одинадцять років, тридцять п'ять років etc.

Learn more about this coordination in this short podcast lesson:
Grammar point: **numeral / noun agreement** in Ukrainian — ukrainianlessons.com/fmu7

How tall are you?	**Якого ви зросту?**	Yakóho vy zróstu?
I am 165 cm tall.	**Один метр шістдесят п'ять сантиметрів.**	Odýn metr shistdesiát piat santymétriv.
one meter	один метр	odýn metr
two meters	два метри	dva métry
one centimeter	один сантиметр	odýn santymétr
two / three / four centimeters	два / три / чотири сантиметри	dva / try / chotýry santymétry
five / six … centimeters	п'ять / шість … сантиметрів	piat / shist … santymétriv

How much money do you have?	**Скільки у вас є грошей?**	Skílky u vas ye hróshei?
How much does it cost?	**Скільки це коштує?**	Skílky tse kóshtuie?
It costs...	**Це коштує...**	Tse kóshtuie...
one dollar	**один долар**	odýn dólar
two / three / four dollars	**два / три / чотири долари**	dva / try / chotýry dólary
five / six ... dollars	**п'ять / шість ... доларів**	piat / shist ... dólariv
one hryvnia	**одну гривню**	odnú hrývniu
two / three / four hryvnias	**дві / три / чотири гривні**	dvi / try / chotýry hrývni
five / six ... hryvnias	**п'ять / шість ... гривень**	piat / shist ... hrýven
one euro	**одне євро**	odné yévro
two / three / four euros	**два / три / чотири євро**	dva / try / chotýry yévro
five / six ... euros	**п'ять / шість ... євро**	piat / shist ... yévro
What is the temperature today?	**Яка сьогодні температура?**	Yaká sohódni temperatúra?
plus	**плюс**	pliús
minus	**мінус**	mínus
one degree	**один градус**	odýn hrádus
two / three / four degrees	**два / три / чотири градуси**	dva / try / chotýry hrádusy
five / six ... degrees	**п'ять / шість ... градусів**	piat / shist ... hrádusiv
twenty-two degrees	**двадцять два градуси**	dvádtsiat dva hrádusy
thirty degrees	**тридцять градусів**	trýdtsiat hrádusiv

What is your phone number?	Який у вас номер телефону?	Yakýi u vas nómer telefónu?
My phone number is 063-427-52-99.	Мій номер телефону - 063-427-52-99 (нуль шістдесят три - чотириста двадцять сім - п'ятдесят два - дев'яносто дев'ять).	Mii nómer telefónu - 063-427-52-99 (nul shistdesiát try - chotýrysta dvádtsiat sim - piatdesiát dva - devianósto déviat).
What is the room number?	Який номер кімнати?	Yakýi nómer kimnáty?
The room number is 480.	Номер кімнати - 480 (чотириста вісімдесят).	Nómer kimnáty - 480 (chotýrysta visimdesiát).
What is the apartment number?	Який номер квартири?	Yakýi nómer kvartýry?
The apartment number is 22.	Номер квартири - 22 (двадцять два).	Nómer kvartýry - 22 (dvádtsiat dva).
What is the house number?	Який номер будинку?	Yakýi nómer budýnku?
The house number is 1246.	Номер будинку - 1246 (тисяча двісті сорок шість).	Nómer budýnku - 1246 (týsiacha dvísti sórok shist).
How many children do you have?	Скільки у вас дітей?	Skílky u vas ditéi?
I have two children.	У мене двоє дітей.	U méne dvóie ditéi.
one child	одна дитина	odná dytýna
two children	двоє дітей	dvóie ditéi
three children	троє дітей	tróie ditéi
four children	четверо дітей	chétvero ditéi
five children	п'ятеро дітей	piátero ditéi

Двоє, троє, четверо are called *collective numerals* and are used with a couple or group of people.

How long have you been in Berlin?	**Як давно ви в Берліні?**	Yak davnó vy v Derlíni?
one day	один день	odýn den
two / three / four days	два / три / чотири дні	dva / try / chotýry dni
five / six … days	п'ять / шість … днів	piat / shist … dniv
one week	один тиждень	odýn týzhden
two / three / four weeks	два / три / чотири тижні	dva / try / chotýry týzhni
five / six … weeks	п'ять / шість … тижнів	piat / shist … týzhniv
one month	один місяць	odýn mísiats
two / three / four months	два / три / чотири місяці	dva / try / chotýry mísiatsi
five / six … months	п'ять / шість … місяців	piat / shist …mísiatsiv
one year	один рік	odýn rik
two / three / four years	два / три / чотири роки	dva / try / chotýry róky
five / six … years	п'ять / шість … років	piat / shist … rókiv

How long will it take?	**Скільки часу це займе?**	Skílky chásu tse zaimé?
It will take…	**Це займе…**	Tse zaimé…
one hour	одну годину	odnú hodýnu
two / three / four hours	дві / три / чотири години	dvi / try / chotýry hodýny
five / six … hours	п'ять / шість … годин	piat / shist … hodýn
one minute	одну хвилину	odnú khvylýnu
two / three / four minutes	дві / три / чотири хвилини	dvi / try / chotýry khvylýny
five / six … minutes	п'ять / шість … хвилин	piat / shist … khvylýn

ordinal numbers	**порядкові числа**	poriadkóvi chýsla
first	перший	pérshyi
second	другий	drúhyi
third	третій	trétii
fourth	четвертий	chetvértyi
fifth	п'ятий	piátyi
sixth	шостий	shóstyi
seventh	сьомий	sómyi
eighth	восьмий	vósmyi
ninth	дев'ятий	deviátyi
tenth	десятий	desiátyi
eleventh	одинадцятий	odynádtsiatyi
twelfth	дванадцятий	dvanádtsiatyi
thirteenth	тринадцятий	trynádtsiatyi
fourteenth	чотирнадцятий	chotyrnádtsiatyi
fifteenth	п'ятнадцятий	piatnádtsiatyi
sixteenth	шістнадцятий	shistnádtsiatyi
seventeenth	сімнадцятий	simnádtsiatyi
eighteenth	вісімнадцятий	visimnádtsiatyi
nineteenth	дев'ятнадцятий	deviatnádtsiatyi
twentieth	двадцятий	dvadtsiátyi
twenty-first	двадцять перший	dvádtsiat pérshyi
thirtieth	тридцятий	trydtsiátyi
fortieth	сороковий	sorokóvyi
fiftieth	п'ятдесятий	piatdesiátyi
hundredth	сотий	sótyi

When did you leave Ukraine?	**Коли ви виїхали з України?**	Kolý vy výikhaly z Ukraíny?
When did you arrive in France?	**Коли ви приїхали у Францію?**	Skílky tse kóshtuie? Frántsiiu?
on the 1st	**першого**	pérshoho
on the 2nd	**другого**	drúhoho
on the 3rd	**третього**	trétoho
on the 4th	**четвертого**	chetvértoho
on the 5th	**п'ятого**	piátoho
on the 6th	**шостого**	shóstoho
on the 7th	**сьомого**	sómoho
on the 8th	**восьмого**	vósmoho
on the 20th	**двадцятого**	dvadtsiátoho
on the 22nd	**двадцять другого**	dvádtsiat drúhoho
on the 30th	**тридцятого**	trydtsiátoho
on the 31st	**тридцять першого**	trýdtsiat pérshoho
of January	**січня**	síchnia
of February	**лютого**	liútoho
of March	**березня**	béreznia
of April	**квітня**	kvítnia
of May	**травня**	trávnia
of June	**червня**	chérvnia
of July	**липня**	lýpnia
of August	**серпня**	sérpnia
of September	**вересня**	véresnia
of October	**жовтня**	zhóvtnia
of November	**листопада**	lystopáda
of December	**грудня**	hrúdnia

2022	дві тисячі двадцять другого року	dvi týsiachi dvádtsiat drúhoho róku
2023	дві тисячі двадцять третього року	dvi týsiachi dvádtsiat trétoho róku
At what time?	**О котрій годині?**	O kotríi hodýni?
At two hours forty-five minutes.	**О другій годині сорок п'ять хвилин.**	O drúhii hodýni sórok piat khvylýn.
hours	**години**	hodýny
one o'clock	**перша година**	pérsha hodýna
two o'clock	**друга година**	drúha hodýna
three o'clock	**третя година**	trétia hodýna
four o'clock	**четверта година**	chetvérta hodýna
five o'clock	**п'ята година**	piáta hodýna
six o'clock	**шоста година**	shósta hodýna
seven o'clock	**сьома година**	sóma hodýna
eight o'clock	**восьма година**	vósma hodýna
nine o'clock	**дев'ята година**	deviáta hodýna
ten o'clock	**десята година**	desiáta hodýna
eleven o'clock	**одинадцята година**	odynádtsiata hodýna
twelve o'clock	**дванадцята година**	dvanádtsiata hodýna
hours	**години**	hodýny
one minute	**одна хвилина**	odná khvylýna
two / three / four minutes	**дві / три / чотири хвилини**	dvi / try / chotýry khvylýny
five / six ... minutes	**п'ять / шість ... хвилин**	piat / shist ... khvylýn

Practice **asking and responding about time** in Ukrainian with this podcast episode: Telling Time — ukrainianlessons.com/episode67

7. Feelings & Emotions

 Link to audio: **ukrainianlessons.com/ph-feelings**

How are...?	Як...?	Yak...?
you (formal or plural)	ви	vy
you (singular informal)	ти	ty
your child	ваша дитина	vásha dytýna
your children	ваші діти	váshi díty
your family	ваша сім'я	vásha simiá
your close ones in Ukraine	ваші близькі в Україні	váshi blyzkí v Ukraíni
Are you okay?	Ви в порядку?	Vy v poriádku?
Is everything okay?	Все гаразд?	Vse harázd?
How are you today?	Як ви сьогодні?	Yak vy sohódni?
How do you feel?	Як ви почуваєтесь?	Yak vy pochuváietes?
Do you feel safe?	Ви почуваєтесь у безпеці?	Vy pochuváietes u bezpétsi?
Are you comfortable?	Вам зручно?	Vam zrúchno?
How can I support you?	Як я можу вас підтримати?	Yak ya mózhu vas pidtrýmaty?
Don't worry.	Не хвилюйтесь.	Ne khvyliúites.
You are safe here.	Тут ви в безпеці.	Tut vy v bezpétsi.
Do you want to talk about this?	Ви хочете про це поговорити?	Vy khóchete pro tse pohovorýty?
Do you want to talk to a psychologist?	Хочете поговорити з психологом?	Khóchete pohovorýty z psykhólohom?
It can help to process trauma.	Це може допомогти пережити травму.	Tse mózhe dopomohtý perezhýty trávmu.

Your mental health is very important.	Ваше психічне здоров'я дуже важливе.	Váshe psykhíchne zdoróvia dúzhe vazhlýve.
It is okay to feel sad and be worried.	Сумувати і хвилюватися — це нормально.	Sumuváty i khvyliuvátysia — tse normálno.
Do you feel...?	Ви відчуваєте...?	Vy vidchuváiete...?
I feel...	Я відчуваю...	Ya vidchuváiu...
anger	гнів	hniv
anxiety	тривогу (from тривога)	tryvóhu (tryvóha)
apathy	апатію (from апатія)	apátiiu (apátiia)
depression	депресію (from депресія)	deprésiiu (deprésiia)
despair	відчай	vídchai
fear	страх	strakh
neurosis	невроз	nevróz
nostalgy	ностальгію (from ностальгія)	nostalhíiu (nostalhíia)
optimism	оптимізм	optymízm
panic	паніку (from паніка)	pániku (pánika)
pessimism	песимізм	pesymízm
sadness	сум	sum
stress	стрес	stres
tiredness	втому (from втома)	vtómu (vtóma)

> Learn different **feelings in Ukrainian** with our infographics and audio:
> Emotions in Ukrainian — **ukrainianlessons.com/emotions**

angry	злий	zlyi
Are you angry?	Ви злі?	Vy zli?
I am very angry. (male / female)	Я дуже злий / зла.	Ya dúzhe zlyi / zla.

awful	жахливий	zhakhlývyi
I feel awful.	Я почуваюсь жахливо.	Ya pochuváius zhakhlývo.
This is awful.	Це жахливо.	Tse zhakhlývo.

brave	хоробрий	khoróbryi
You are very brave.	Ви дуже хоробрі.	Vy dúzhe khoróbri.
This is a very brave act.	Це дуже хоробрий вчинок.	Tse dúzhe khoróbryi vchýnok.

calm	спокійний	spokíinyi
Are you calm?	Ви спокійні?	Vy spokíini?
I am calm. (male / female)	Я спокійний / спокійна.	Ya spokíinyi / spokíina.

confident	впевнений	vpévnenyi
Do you feel confident?	Ви почуваєтесь впевнено?	Vy pochuváietes vpévneno?
I am confident that... (male / female)	Я впевнений / впевнена, що...	Ya vpévnenyi / vpévnena, shcho...

distressed	засмучений	zasmúchenyi
Are you distressed?	Ви засмучені?	Vy zasmúcheni?
I am distressed. (male / female)	Я засмучений / засмучена.	Ya zasmúchenyi / zasmúchena.

glad	радий	rádyi
Are you glad?	Ви раді?	Vy rádi?
I am glad. (male / female)	Я радий / рада.	Ya rádyi / ráda.

grumpy	**сердитий**	serdýtyi
Are you grumpy?	Ви сердиті?	Vy serdýti?
I am grumpy. (male / female)	Я сердитий / сердита.	Ya serdýtyi / serdýta.

happy	**щасливий**	shchaslývyi
Are you happy?	Ви щасливі?	Vy shchaslývi?
I am happy. (male / female)	Я щасливий / щаслива.	Ya shchaslývyi / shchaslýva.

irritated	**роздратований**	rozdratóvanyi
Are you irritated?	Ви роздратовані?	Vy rozdratóvani?
I am irritated. (male / female)	Я роздратований / роздратована.	Ya rozdratóvanyi / rozdratóvana.

miserable	**нещасний**	neshchásnyi
Are you miserable?	Ви нещасні?	Vy neshchásni?
I am miserable. (male / female)	Я нещасний / нещасна.	Ya neshchásnyi / neshchásna.

satisfied	**задоволений**	zadovólenyi
Are you satisfied?	Ви задоволені?	Vy zadovóleni?
I am satisfied. (male / female)	Я задоволений / задоволена.	Ya zadovólenyi / zadovólena.

surprised	**здивований**	zdyvóvanyi
Are you surprised?	Ви здивовані?	Vy zdyvóvani?
I am surprised. (male / female)	Я здивований / здивована.	Ya zdyvóvanyi / zdyvóvana.

tired	**втомлений**	vtómlenyi
Are you tired?	Ви втомлені?	Vy vtómleni?
I am tired. (male / female)	Я втомлений / втомлена.	Ya vtómlenyi / vtómlena.

to cry	**плакати**	plákaty
Do you often cry?	**Ви часто плачете?**	Vy chásto pláchete?
I cry a lot.	**Я багато плачу.**	Ya baháto pláchu.
to be nervous	**нервуватись**	nervuvátys
Are you nervous?	**Ви нервуєтесь?**	Vy nervúietes?
I am nervous.	**Я нервуюсь.**	Ya nervúius.
to be proud	**пишатись**	pyshátys
Are you proud?	**Ви пишаєтесь?**	Vy pysháietes?
I am proud of you.	**Я пишаюсь вами.**	Ya pysháius vámy.
to be sad	**сумувати (сумно)**	sumuváty (súmno)
Are you sad?	**Вам сумно?**	Vam súmno?
I am sad.	**Мені сумно.**	Mení súmno.
to be scared	**боятися (страшно)**	boiátysia (stráshno)
Are you scared?	**Вам страшно?**	Vam stráshno?
I am scared.	**Мені страшно.**	Mení stráshno.
to worry	**хвилюватись**	khvyliuvátys
Are you worried about them?	**Ви хвилюєтесь за них?**	Vy khvyliúietes za nykh?
I am very worried.	**Я дуже хвилююсь.**	Ya dúzhe khvyliúius.

8. Giving Support

 Link to audio: ukrainianlooooono.com/ph_support

Take care!	**Бережи себе!**	Berezhý sebé!
	Бережіть себе!*	Berezhít sebé!*
Hang in there!	**Тримайся!**	Trymáisia!
	Тримайтесь!*	Trymáites!*

I...	**Я...**	Ya...
think about you	**думаю про тебе (вас)***	dúmaiu pro tébe (vas)
worry a lot about you	**дуже хвилююсь за тебе (вас)***	dúzhe khvyliúius za tébe (vas)
love you very much	**дуже люблю тебе (вас)***	dúzhe liubliú tebé (vas)
pray for you	**молюся за тебе (вас)***	moliúsia za tébe (vas)

We...	**Ми...**	My...
think about you	**думаємо про тебе (вас)***	dúmaiemo pro tébe (vas)
worry a lot about you	**дуже хвилюємось за тебе (вас)***	dúzhe khvyliúiemos za tébe (vas)
love you very much	**дуже любимо тебе (вас)***	dúzhe liúbymo tebé (vas)
pray for you	**молимося за тебе (вас)***	mólymosia za tébe (vas)

*The first variant is addressed towards one person. The second one is towards many people or one person in a more formal way.

Welcome.	Ласкаво просимо.	Laskávo prósymo.
You are safe here.	Тут ви в безпеці.	Tut vy v bezpétsi.
There is hope.	Надія є.	Nadíia ye.
Everything will be fine.	Усе буде добре.	Usé búde dóbre.
I am nearby.	Я поруч.	Ya póruch.
I am with you.	Я з тобою (вами).	Ya z tobóiu (vámy).

Is everything fine with you?	У вас усе добре?	U vas usé dóbre?
How is your health?	Як ваше здоров'я?	Yak váshe zdoróvia?
How can I help?	Як я можу допомогти?	Yak ya mózhu dopomohtý?
What is your news?	Які у вас новини?	Yakí u vas novýny?

Glory to Ukraine!	Слава Україні!	Sláva Ukraíni!
Glory to Heroes!	Героям Слава!	Heróiam Sláva!
Ukraine is in my heart.	Україна в моєму серці.	Ukraína v moiému sértsi.
Everything will be Ukraine!	Все буде Україна!	Vse búde Ukraína!
(Insert your country) is with you!	(...) з вами!	(...) z vámy!

Come back alive and healthy! (to a soldier)	Повертайся живим і здоровим!	Povertáisia zhyvým i zdoróvym!
May he come back alive and healthy!	Нехай повертається живим і здоровим!	Nekhái povertáietsia zhyvým i zdoróvym!
God save you (him, them...)!	Хай Бог береже!	Khai Boh berezhé!
My prayers are with Ukraine.	Мої молитви з Україною.	Moí molytvý z Ukraínoiu.

9. Language & Communication

 Link to audio: **ukrainianlessons.com/ph-language**

I don't understand.	**Я не розумію.**	Ya ne rozumíiu.
I don't understand any of it.	Я нічого не розумію.	Ya nichóho ne rozumíiu.
I don't understand all of it.	Я не все розумію.	Ya ne vse rozumíiu.
I still don't understand.	Я все одно не розумію.	Ya vse odnó ne rozumíiu.
I understand all of it.	Я все розумію.	Ya vse rozumíiu.
Do you understand?	Ви розумієте?	Vy rozumíiete?

Could you please...?	**Можете, будь ласка...?**	Mózhete, bud láska...?
repeat	повторити	povtorýty
talk slowly	розмовляти повільно	rozmovliáty povílno
say it slowly	сказати це повільно	skazáty tse povílno
write it down	записати це	zapysáty tse
write in Google Translate	записати в Google перекладачі	zapysáty v Góogle perekladachí

Do you speak...?	**Ви розмовляєте...?**	Vy rozmovliáiete...?
English	англійською	anhlíiskoiu
Polish	польською	pólskoiu
Czech	чеською	chéskoiu
German	німецькою	nimétskoiu
Italian	італійською	italíiskoiu
Ukrainian	українською	ukraínskoiu
Russian	російською	rosíiskoiu
other languages	іншими мовами	ínshymy móvamy

I speak Ukrainian a little bit.	Я трошки розмовляю українською.	Ya tróshky rozmovliáiu ukraínskoiu.
I don't speak Russian, but I speak a little bit of Ukrainian.	Я не розмовляю російською, але я трошки розмовляю українською.	Ya ne rozmovliáiu rosíiskoiu, alé ya tróshky rozmovliáiu ukraínskoiu.
I am learning Ukrainian.	Я вивчаю українську мову.	Ya vyvcháiu ukraínsku móvu.
I don't speak Ukrainian very well yet.	Я ще не дуже добре розмовляю українською.	Ya shche ne dúzhe dóbre rozmovliáiu ukraínskoiu.
You can correct my mistakes.	Ви можете виправляти мої помилки.	Vy mózhete vypravliáty moí pomylký.
How do you say it?	Як це сказати?	Yak tse skazáty?
What do you call this in Ukrainian?	Як це називається українською?	Yak tse nazyváietsia ukraínskoiu?
What does this word mean?	Що означає це слово?	Shcho oznacháie tse slóvo?
How do you spell your name?	Як пишеться ваше ім'я?	Yak pýshetsia váshe imiá?
How do you pronounce this correctly?	Як правильно це вимовити?	Yak právylno tse výmovyty?
Did I say it right? (male / female)	Я правильно це сказав / сказала?	Ya právylno tse skazáv / skazála?
Thank you for helping me learn Ukrainian.	Дякую, що допомагаєте мені вивчати українську мову.	Diákuiu, shcho dopomaháiete mení vyvcháty ukraínsku móvu.

I don't know how to say it in Ukrainian.	Я не знаю, як сказати це українською.	Ya ne znáiu, yak skazáty tse ukraínskoiu.
I will be using Google translate.	Я буду користуватися Google перекладачем.	Ya búdu korystuvátysia Góogle perekladachém.
We can use Google translate on my phone / tablet and communicate this way.	Ми можемо користуватися Google перекладачем на моєму телефоні / планшеті, і так спілкуватися.	My mózhemo korystuvátysia Góogle perekladachém na moiému telefóni / planshéti, i tak spilkuvátysia.
Can you find what you want to say here [in this phrasebook]?	Ви можете знайти тут, що ви хочете сказати?	Vy mózhete znaitý tut, shcho vy khóchete skazáty?
Write down a list of things you need in Ukrainian.	Напишіть, будь ласка, українською мовою список речей, які вам потрібні.	Napyshít, bud láska, ukraínskoiu móvoiu spýsok rechéi, yakí vam potríbni.

Learn some of **the most useful phrases for your Ukrainian learning**
in this 5 Minute Ukrainian lesson:
Useful phrases for learning Ukrainian — ukrainianlessons.com/fmu2

Google Translate is definitely very useful for quick communication in any language.
It is not always accurate, but it will probably help you pass your message.
Here are some other **useful online dictionaries/services** for your Ukrainian learning:

Ukrainian dictionary (definitions, conjugation, synonyms, etc.) — goroh.pp.ua
Different languages — Ukrainian dictionaries — glosbe.com
English — Ukrainian dictionaries — e2u.org.ua
Spelling check — r2u.org.ua/check
Automatic transliteration — slovnyk.ua/translit.php
Automatic word stressing — slovnyk.ua/nagolos.php

This is...	Це —	Tse —
my phone number	мій номер телефону	mii nómer telefónu
my email	мій імейл	mii iméil
my business card	моя візитка	moiá vizýtka
Do you have...?	У вас є...?	U vas ye...?
phone	телефон	telefón
sim card	SIM-карта	SIM-kárta
email address	електронна адреса	elektrónna adrésa
Are you...?	Ви є...	Vy ye...
on Facebook	у Фейсбуці?	u Feisbútsi?
on Instagram	в Інстаграмі?	v Instahrámi?
on Viber	у Вайбері?	u Váiberi?
on Whatsapp	у Вотсапі?	u Votsápi?
on Telegram	у Телеграмі?	u Telehrámi?
You can...	Ви можете...	Vy mózhete...
call me	дзвонити мені	dzvonýty mení
video call me	дзвонити мені з відео	dzvonýty mení z vídeo
text me	писати мені повідомлення	pysáty mení povidómlennia
email me	писати мені на імейл	pysáty mení na iméil

Are you an active user of **social media**? Listen to this podcast episode to practice:
Talking about social media in Ukrainian — ukrainianlessons.com/episode53

And make sure to **subscribe** :)
Ukrainian Lessons on Facebook — facebook.com/ukrainianlessons
Ukrainian Lessons on Instagram — instagram.com/ukrainianlessons
Ukrainian Lessons on Twitter — twitter.com/ukrlessons

---

10. Around the house

 Link to audio: **ukrainianlessons.com/ph-house**

Welcome.	Ласкаво просимо.	Laskávo prósymo.
Make yourself / yourselves at home.	Почувайтесь, як вдома.	Pochuváites, yak vdóma.
Can I help you with the bag?	Я можу допомогти вам із сумкою?	Ya mózhu dopomohtý vam iz súmkoiu?
Is there anything you need?	Вам щось потрібно?	Vam shchos potríbno?
What do you want to do?	Що ви хочете робити?	Shcho vy khóchete robýty?
Where do you want to go?	Куди ви хочете піти?	Kudý vy khóchete pitý?
When do you need to wake up?	Коли вам потрібно прокинутися?	Kolý vam potríbno prokýnutysia?
Please, don't be shy.	Будь ласка, не соромтесь.	Bud láska, ne sorómtes.
If you need anything, just let me know.	Якщо вам щось потрібно, тільки скажіть.	Yakshchó vam shchos potríbno, tílky skazhít.
Do you want to join us?	Хочете приєднатися до нас?	Khóchete pryiednátysia do nas?
Do you think you can do this / go there by yourself / yourselves?	Ви думаєте, ви можете зробити це / поїхати туди самостійно?	Vy dúmaiete, vy mózhete zrobýty tse / poíkhaty tudý samostíino?
It doesn't work.	Це не працює.	Tse ne pratsiúie.

Would you like to...?	Хочете...?	Khóchete...?
have breakfast (together)	поснідати (разом)	posnídaty (razom)
have lunch (together)	пообідати (разом)	poobídaty (razom)
have dinner (together)	повечеряти (разом)	povechériaty (razom)
go for a walk (together)	погуляти (разом)	pohuliáty (razom)
watch TV (together)	подивитися телевізор (разом)	podyvýtysia televízor (razom)
go to the park	піти в парк	pitý v park
go to the store	піти в магазин	pitý v mahazýn
come with me (by walking / by transport)	піти / поїхати зі мною	pitý / poíkhaty zi mnóiu
come with us (by walking / by transport)	піти / поїхати з нами	pitý / poíkhaty z námy

You can...	Ви можете...	Vy mózhete...
take any food from the refrigerator	брати будь-яку їжу з холодильника	bráty bud-yakú yízhu z kholodýlnyka
cook in the kitchen	готувати на кухні	hotuváty na kúkhni
make yourself / yourselves tea or coffee	готувати собі чай чи каву	hotuváty sobí chai chy kávu
take a shower	приймати душ	pryimáty dush
take a bath	приймати ванну	pryimáty vánnu
take towels here	брати рушники тут	bráty rushnyký tut
machine wash clothes	прати одяг в машинці	práty ódiah v mashýntsi
watch TV	дивитись телевізор	dyvýtys televízor
use a computer	користуватись комп'ютером	korystuvátys kompiúterom

housing	**житло**	zhytló
house	**будинок**	budýnok
apartment	**квартира**	kvartýra
room	**кімната**	kimnáta

house	**будинок**	budýnok
attic	**горище**	horýshche
backyard	**задній двір**	zádnii dvir
basement	**підвал**	pidvál
balcony	**балкон**	balkón
door	**двері**	dvéri
downstairs	**внизу**	vnyzú
entrance	**вхід**	vkhid
floor	**підлога**	pidlóha
front yard	**передній двір**	perédnii dvir
garage	**гараж**	harázh
garden	**сад**	sad
hall	**коридор**	korydór
parking	**парковка**	parkóvka
porch	**веранда**	veránda
roof	**дах**	dakh
stairway	**сходи**	skhódy
upstairs	**нагорі**	nahorí
wall	**стіна**	stiná
window	**вікно**	viknó

> Listen to this short lesson for all the necessary words for types of **housing and rooms in Ukrainian**: Housing Vocabulary Booster — <u>ukrainianlessons.com/fmu42</u>

rooms	кімнати	kimnáty
bathroom	ванна кімната	vánna kimnáta
bedroom	спальня	spálnia
guest room	гостьова кімната	hostová kimnáta
hall	коридор	korydór
kitchen	кухня	kúkhnia
living room	зал	zal
toilet	туалет	tualét

things in the kitchen	речі на кухні	réchi na kúkhni
bowl	миска	mýska
chopping board	дошка	dóshka
coffee machine	кавоварка	kavovárka
colander	сито	sýto
corkscrew	штопор	shtópor
cup, mug	чашка	cháshka
dishes	посуд	pósud
dishtowel	кухонний рушник	kukhónnyi rushnýk
dishwasher	посудомийка	posudomýika
fork	виделка	vydélka
frying pan	сковорідка	skovorídka
garbage can	смітник	smitnýk
garbage disposal	подрібнювач відходів	podríbniuvach vidkhódiv
glass	склянка	skliánka
grater	тертка	tértka
kettle	чайник	cháinyk
kitchen cabinet	шафка	sháfka
kitchen sink	раковина	rákovyna

knife	ніж	nizh
ladle	черпак	cherpák
microwave	мікрохвильовка	mikrokhvylóvka
napkin	серветка	servétka
oven	духовка	dukhóvka
plate	тарілка	tarílka
pot	каструля	kastrúlia
refrigerator	холодильник	kholodýlnyk
spatula	лопатка	lopátka
sponge	губка	húbka
spoon	ложка	lózhka
stove	плита	plytá
table	стіл	stil
toaster	тостер	tóster

things in the bathroom	речі у ванній	réchi u vánnii
bathtub	ванна	vánna
comb	гребінець	hrebinéts
cream	крем	krem
detergent	засіб для прання	zásib dlia panniá
dryer	сушильна машина	sushýlna mashýna
faucet	кран	kran
hairbrush	щітка для волосся	shchítka dlia volóssia
razor	бритва	brýtva
sanitary pads	прокладки	prokládky
shampoo	шампунь	shampún
shower	душ	dush
shower curtain	шторка для душу	shtórka dlia dúshu

soap	мило	mýlo
tampons	тампони	tampóny
toilet bowl	унітаз	unitáz
toilet paper	туалетний папір	tualétnyi papír
toilet seat	кришка унітаза	krýshka unitáza
toothbrush	зубна щітка	zubná shchítka
toothpaste	зубна паста	zubná pásta
towel	рушник	rushnýk
washing machine	пральна машина	prálna mashýna
water heater	бойлер	bóiler
things in the room	**речі в кімнаті**	**réchi v kimnáti**
armchair	крісло	kríslo
bed	ліжко	lízhko
blinds	жалюзі	zhaliuzí
(book) shelf	(книжкова) полиця	(knyzhkóva) polýtsia
carpet	килим	kýlym
chair	стілець	stiléts
closet, wardrobe	шафа	sháfa
coffee table	столик	stólyk
curtains	штори	shtóry
dresser	комод	komód
furniture	меблі	mébli
lamp	лампа	lámpa
mirror	дзеркало	dzérkalo
radiator	батарея	bataréia
sofa	диван	dyván
table	стіл	stil

bed linen	постільна білизна	postílna bilýzna
blanket	ковдра	kóvdra
mattress	матрац	matráts
pillow	подушка	podúshka
pillowcase	наволочка	návolochka
roll mat	каремат	karemát
sheet	простирадло	prostyrádlo
sleeping bag	спальник	spálnyk

cleaning	прибирання	prybyránnia
broom	віник	vínyk
dustpan	совок	sovók
mop	швабра	shvábra
vacuum cleaner	пилосос	pylosós

Curious to learn how to talk about **cleaning in Ukrainian**?
Check out this short dialogue lesson:
Cleaning & Tidying — ukrainianlessons.com/fmu45

other things	інші речі	ínshi réchi
charger	зарядка	zariádka
computer	комп'ютер	kompiúter
key	ключ	kliuch
light bulb	лампочка	lámpochka
lock	замок	zamók
plug socket	розетка	rozétka
scissors	ножиці	nózhytsi
TV	телевізор	televízor

If you are hosting Ukrainians, this vocabulary booster will be particularly useful for you:
Things you can find in every house — ukrainianlessons.com/fmu44

11. Places & Navigation

 Link to audio: ukrainianlessons.com/ph-places

Where? (location)	**Де?**	De?
Where to? (direction)	**Куди?**	Kudý?
Where is it?	Де це?	De tse?
Where are you going?	Куди ви йдете?	Kudý vy ydeté?
Where do you need to go?	Куди вам треба?	Kudý vam tréba?
Let's go.	Ходімо.	Khodímo.
Wait.	Зачекайте.	Zachekáite.
Come here.	Ідіть сюди.	Idít siudý.
It is that way.	Це в той бік.	Tse v toi bik.
Come with me.	Ходімо зі мною.	Khodímo zi mnóiu.
I will show you where it is.	Я покажу вам, де це.	Ya pokazhú vam, de tse.
Do you have a map on your phone?	У вас є карта на телефоні?	U vas ye kárta na telefóni?
I will make an itinerary for you.	Я прокладу вам маршрут.	Ya prokladú vam marshrút.
You need to go here.	Вам треба сюди.	Vam tréba siudý.
Here is this place.	Ось це місце.	Os tse místse.
Cross the street.	Перейдіть вулицю.	Pereidít vúlytsiu.
Walk down the street...	Ідіть по вулиці...	Idít po vúlytsi...
Can I give you a ride somewhere?	Я можу вас кудись підвезти?	Ya mózhu vas kudýs pidveztý?
We can go there by car.	Ми можемо поїхати туди на машині.	My mózhemo poíkhaty tudý na mashýni.
I will drive you there.	Я завезу вас туди.	Ya zavezú vas tudý.

town, city	**місто**	místo
in the town, in the city	у місті	u místi
village	**село**	seló
in the village	у селі	u selí
street	**вулиця**	vúlytsia
on the street	на вулиці	na vúlytsi
Go...	**Ідіть...**	Idít...
straight	прямо	priámo
Turn...	**Поверніть...**	Povernít...
left	ліворуч	livóruch
right	праворуч	pravóruch

Practice **giving directions in context** in the episode #18 of Ukrainian Lessons Podcast: Directions in Ukrainian — <u>ukrainianlessons.com/episode18</u>

It is...	**Це...**	Tse...
here	тут	tut
there	там	tam
right here	ось тут	os tut
over there	он там	on tam
far	далеко	daléko
not far	не далеко	ne daléko
two kilometers from here	за два кілометри звідси	za dva kilométry zvídsy
three blocks from here	за три квартали звідси	za try kvartály zvídsy
a 10-minute walk from here	за десять хвилин пішки звідси	za désiat khvylýn píshky zvídsy
a 5-minute ride from here	за п'ять хвилин їзди звідси	za piát khvylýn yizdý zvídsy

Do you know where... is?	Ви знаєте, де... ?	Vy znáiete, de... ?
airport	аеропорт	aeropórt
bank	банк	bank
bookstore	книжковий магазин	knyzhkóvyi mahazýn
bus station	автовокзал	avtovokzál
bus stop	автобусна зупинка	avtóbusna zupýnka
church	церква	tsérkva
city center	центр міста	tsentr místa
city hall	мерія	mériia
clinic	клініка	klínika
fire station	пожежна станція	pozhézhna stántsiia
gas station	заправка	zaprávka
grocery store	магазин продуктів	mahazýn prodúktiv
harbor	порт	port
hospital	лікарня	likárnia
hotel	готель	hotél
kindergarten	дитячий садок	dytiáchyi sadók
laundromat	пральня	prálnia
library	бібліотека	bibliotéka
mosque	мечеть	mechét
movie theater	кінотеатр	kinoteátr
museum	музей	muzéi
pharmacy	аптека	aptéka
police station	поліція	polítsiia
post office	пошта	póshta
railway station	залізничний вокзал	zaliznýchnyi vokzál
restaurant	ресторан	restorán

school	школа	shkóla
elementary school	початкова школа	pochatkóva shkóla
middle school	середня школа	serédnia shkóla
high school	старша школа	stársha shkóla
subway station	станція метро	stántsiia metró
supermarket	супермаркет	supermárket
thrift shop	комісійний магазин	komisíinyi mahazýn
train station	залізничний вокзал	zaliznýchnyi vokzál
tram stop	трамвайна зупинка	tramváina zupýnka
unemployment office	центр зайнятості	tsentr záiniatosti

transport	**транспорт**	**tránsport**
ambulance	швидка допомога	shvydká dopomóha
bicycle	велосипед	velosypéd
boat	човен	chóven
bus	автобус	avtóbus
car	машина, авто	mashýna, avtó
helicopter	гелікоптер	helikoptér
motorcycle	мотоцикл	mototsýkl
plane	літак	liták
ship	корабель	korabél
taxi	таксі	taksí
train	поїзд	póizd
tram	трамвай	tramvái
truck	вантажівка, фура	vantazhívka, fúra
van	фургон	furhón

Transport Vocabulary Booster — ukrainianlessons.com/fmu4
Choosing the **best way** to go to Lviv — ukrainianlessons.com/fmu5

---

12. Health

 Link to audio: ukrainianlessons.com/ph-health

Do you need any medical help?	Вам потрібна медична допомога?	Vam potríbna medýchna dopomóha?
Are you all right?	Ви в порядку?	Vy v poriádku?
How do you feel?	Як ви почуваєтесь?	Yak vy pochuváietes?
Do you need a doctor?	Вам потрібен лікар?	Vam potríben líkar?
Do you need to see a doctor?	Вам потрібно звернутися до лікаря?	Vam potríbno zvernútysia do líkaria?
Do you want to go to the hospital?	Хочете поїхати в лікарню?	Khóchete poíkhaty v likárniu?
Would you like to see a psychologist?	Ви б хотіли звернутися до психолога?	Vy b khotíly zvernútysia do psykhóloha?
Do you have any illnesses?	У вас є якісь хвороби?	U vas ye yakís khvoróby?
Do you have any health conditions?	У вас є якісь особливості здоров'я?	U vas ye yakís osoblývosti zdoróvia?
Are you pregnant?	Ви вагітні?	Vy vahítni?
Have you been raped?	Вас зґвалтували?	Vas zgvaltuvály?
Are you healthy (in general)?	Ви здорові (загалом)?	Vy zdoróvi (zahalóm)?
Is your child healthy?	Ваша дитина здорова?	Vásha dytýna zdoróva?
Are your children healthy?	Ваші діти здорові?	Váshi díty zdoróvi?

symptoms	**симптоми**	symptómy
Where does it hurt?	**Де у вас болить?**	De u vas bolýt?
Are you in pain?	**Вам боляче?**	Vam bóliache?
Are you injured?	**Ви поранені?**	Vy poráneni?
How long has it been hurting?	**Як довго це у вас болить?**	Yak dóvho tse u vas bolýt?
Have you ever had this before?	**У вас було таке раніше?**	U vas búlo také raníshe?
Do you have an appetite?	**У вас є апетит?**	U vas ye apetýt?
How do you sleep?	**Як ви спите?**	Yak vy spyté?
What is your bowel movement like?	**Як ваші випорожнення?**	Yak váshi výporozhnennia?
Do you feel dizzy?	**У вас крутиться в голові?**	U vas krútytsia v holoví?

Do you have...? I have...	**У вас є...? У мене...**	U vas ye...? U méne...
fever	**температура**	temperatúra
allergy	**алергія**	alerhíia
arthritis	**артрит**	artrýt
asthma	**астма**	ástma
bleeding	**кровотеча**	krovotécha
lice	**воші**	vóshi
cancer	**рак**	rak
cold	**застуда**	zastúda
constipation	**запор**	zapór
coronavirus	**коронавірус**	koronavírus
cough	**кашель**	káshel

diabetes	діабет	diabét
diarrhea	діарея	diaréia
flu	грип	hryp
gastric problems	проблеми зі шлунком	problémy zi shlúnkom
headache	головний біль	holovnýi bil
heart problems	проблеми з серцем	problémy z sértsem
inflammation	запалення	zapálennia
nausea	нудота	nudóta
pain	біль	bil
sore throat	біль у горлі	bil u hórli
stomachache	біль у шлунку	bil u shlúnku
toothache	зубний біль	zubnýi bil
tuberculosis	туберкульоз	tuberkulóz
ulcer	виразка	výrazka
vomiting	блювота	bliuvóta

Do you have...?	У вас болить...?	U vas bolýt...?
I have...	У мене болить...	U méne bolýt...
headache	голова	holová
sore throat	горло	hórlo
stomachache	шлунок	shlúnok
toothache	зуб	zub

Listen to some **common conversations about being sick** in these podcast episodes:
I don't feel good — ukrainianlessons.com/episode101
Making a doctor's appointment — ukrainianlessons.com/episode102
At the doctor's — ukrainianlessons.com/episode103
Healthy lifestyle — ukrainianlessons.com/episode104

body	тіло	tílo
abdomen	живіт	zhyvít
ankle	щиколотка	shchýkolotka
arm	рука	ruká
back	спина	spýna
bladder	сечовий міхур	sechovýi mikhúr
blood	кров	krov
bones	кістки	kistký
chest	грудна клітина	hrudná klitýna
ears	вуха	vúkha
elbow	лікоть	líkot
eyes	очі	óchi
face	обличчя	oblýchchia
finger	палець руки	pálets rúky
foot	стопа	stopá
forehead	лоб	lob
hair	волосся	volóssia
hand	долоня	dolónia
head	голова	holová
heart	серце	sértse
hips	стегна	stéhna
intestines	кишківник	kyshkivnýk
kidneys	нирки	nýrky
knee	коліно	kolíno
leg	нога	nohá
liver	печінка	pechínka
lungs	легені	lehéni

mouth	рот	rot
muscle	м'яз	miaz
nail	ніготь	níhot
neck	шия	shýia
nose	ніс	nis
shoulder	плече	pleché
skin	шкіра	shkíra
stomach	шлунок	shlúnok
teeth	зуби	zúby
toe	палець ноги	pálets nohý
tongue	язик	yazýk
waist	талія	táliia
wrist	зап'ястя	zapiástia

Body parts Vocabulary Booster – ukrainianlessons.com/fmu52

COVID	ковід, коронавірус	kóvid, koronavírus
COVID vaccine	вакцина проти коронавірусу	vaktsýna próty koronavírusu
vaccination certificate	сертифікат про вакцинацію	sertyfikát pro vaktsynátsiiu
coronavirus symptoms	симптоми коронавірусу	symptómy koronavírusu
antigen test	тест на антиген	test na antyhén
PCR-Test	ПЛР-тест	PLR-test
Are you vaccinated?	Ви вакциновані?	Vy vaktsynóvani?
Do you want to get a vaccine?	Ви бажаєте вакцинуватися?	Vy bazháiete vaktsynuvátysia?
Please wear a mask.	Надіньте маску, будь ласка.	Nadínte másku, bud láska.

pregnancy	**вагітність**	vahítnist
When was your last menstrual period?	**Коли була ваша остання менструація?**	Kolý bulá vasha ostánnia menstruátsiia?
Have you been pregnant before?	**Ви вже були вагітні?**	Vy vzhe bulý vahítni?
How many weeks / months pregnant are you?	**На якому ви тижні / місяці вагітності?**	Na yakómu vy týzhni / mísiatsi vahítnosti?
How often do you have contractions?	**Як часто у вас перейми?**	Yak chásto u vas peréimy?

medications	**ліки**	líky
Are you taking any medicine?	**Ви приймаєте якісь ліки?**	Vy pryimáiete yakís líky?
Do you need medicine?	**Вам потрібні ліки?**	Vam potríbni líky?
Do you need some special medications?	**Вам потрібні спеціальні ліки?**	Vam potríbni petsiálni líky?
Do you have a list of your medications?	**У вас є список ваших ліків?**	U vas ye spýsok váshykh líkiv?
What medications do you take?	**Які ліки ви приймаєте?**	Yakí líky vy pryimáiete?
Do you understand the instructions for the medications?	**Ви розумієте інструкції до ліків?**	Vy rozumíiete instrúktsii do líkiv?
Do you need a prescription?	**Вам потрібен рецепт?**	Vam potríben retsépt?
You need a prescription for these medications.	**Вам потрібен рецепт на ці ліки.**	Vam potríben retsépt na tsi líky.

ambulance	швидка допомога	shvydká dopomóha
bandage	бинт	bynt
chemotherapy	хіміотерапія	khimioterapíia
cotton wool	вата	váta
crutches	милиці	mýlytsi
plaster	пластир	plástyr
vitamins	вітаміни	vitamíny
wet wipes	вологі серветки	volóhi servétky
wheelchair	інвалідний візок	invalídnyi vizók
ointment	мазь	maz
tablets	таблетки	tablétky
nasal spray	спрей для носа	sprei dlia nósa
cough syrup	сироп проти кашлю	syróp próty káshliu

doctor	лікар	líkar
cardiologist	кардіолог	kardióloh
dentist	стоматолог	stomatóloh
gynecologist	гінеколог	hinekóloh
obstetrician	акушер	akushér
ophthalmologist	окуліст	okulíst
pediatrician	педіатр	pediátr
pharmacist	аптекар	aptékar
psychiatrist	психіатр	psykhiátr
psychologist	психолог	psykhóloh
surgeon	хірург	khirúrh

13. Food

 Link to audio: ukrainianlessons.com/ph-food

Would you like ...?	Ви хочете ... ?	Vy khóchete ... ?
to eat	їсти	yísty
to drink	пити	pýty
to take some food	взяти їжу	vziáty yízhu
to have a snack	перекусити	perekusýty
to have breakfast	поснідати	posnídaty
to have lunch	пообідати	poobídaty
to have dinner	повечеряти	povechériaty
a cup of tea	чашку чаю	cháshku cháiu
some water	води	vodý

Here you go.	Ось, будь ласка.	Os, bud láska.
Enjoy your meal!	Смачного!	Smachnóho!
Did you like it?	Вам сподобалося?	Vam spodóbalosia?
Do you want some more?	Хочете ще?	Khóchete shche?
Please have some more.	Будь ласка, візьміть ще.	Bud láska, vizmít shche.
Do you have enough to eat?	У вас достатньо їжі?	U vas dostátno yízhi?
Please line up here.	Будь ласка, станьте в чергу тут.	Bud láska, stánte v chérhu tut.
Children first.	Спочатку діти.	Spochátku díty.
Then women.	Потім жінки.	Pótim zhinký.

We have ...	У нас є ...	U nas ye ...
food	їжа	yízha
bread	хліб	khlib
cake	торт	tort
candies	цукерки	tsukérky
cheese	сир	syr
chicken	курка	kúrka
cookies	печиво	péchyvo
eggs	яйця	yáitsia
fish	риба	rýba
fruit	фрукти	frúkty
meat	м'ясо	miáso
omelet	омлет	omlét
pasta	паста	pásta
pizza	піца	pítsa
pork	свинина	svynýna
porridge	каша	kásha
potatoes	картопля	kartóplia
rice	рис	rys
salad	салат	salát
sandwich	бутерброд	buterbród
scrambled eggs	яєчня	yaiéchnia
soup	суп	sup
veal	телятина	teliátyna
vegetables	овочі	óvochi
yogurt	йогурт	yóhurt

Practice **talking about food using genitive case** with this episode of
Ukrainian Lessons Podcast:
At the grocery store — **ukrainianlessons.com/episode46**

drinks	**напої**	napói
coffee	кава	káva
with sugar	з цукром	z tsúkrom
without sugar	без цукру	bez tsúkru
juice	сік	sik
milk	молоко	molokó
lactose-free milk	безлактозне молоко	bezlaktózne molokó
soft drink	газований напій	hazóvanyi napíi
tea	чай	chai
water	вода	vodá

Listen to a **real conversation in one of the Kyiv's hipster coffee shops**
in this podcast episode:
Ordering drinks in Ukrainian — **ukrainianlessons.com/episode11**

---

describing food	**опис їжі**	ópys yízhi
bitter	гіркий	hirkýi
cold	холодний	kholódnyi
fresh	свіжий	svízhyi
hot	гарячий	hariáchyi
salty	солоний	solónyi
sour	кислий	kýslyi
spicy / hot	гострий	hóstryi
sweet	солодкий	solódkyi
tasty, delicious	смачний	smachnýi
warm	теплий	téplyi

Remember to use appropriate endings for different genders and plural forms:
смачн**ий** торт, смачн**а** піца, смачн**е** яблуко, смачн**і** цукерки

What do you like to eat for ...?	**Що ви любите їсти на...?**	Shcho vy liúbyte yísty na...?.
breakfast	снідаНок	snidánok
lunch	обід	obíd
dinner	вечерю	vechériu
dessert	десерт	desért

Have you had ... yet?	**Ви вже ...?**	Vy vzhe ...?
breakfast	снідали	snídaly
lunch	обідали	obídaly
dinner	вечеряли	vechérialy

special dietary needs	**особливі дієтичні потреби**	osoblývi diietýchni potréby
Is there something you don't eat?	Чи є щось, що ви не їсте?	Chy ye shchos, shcho vy ne yisté?
Do you eat meat?	Ви їсте м'ясо?	Vy yisté miáso?
Are you allergic to something?	У вас є алергія на щось?	U vas ye alerhíia na shchos?
I am a vegetarian. (male / female)	Я вегетаріанець / вегетаріанка.	Ya vehetariánets / vehetariánka.
I am a vegan. (male / female)	Я веган / веганка.	Ya vehán / vehánka.

If you are ready to listen to a podcast in 100% slow Ukrainian, check out these **episodes for foodies**:
Lent and Ukrainian vegan dishes — <u>ukrainianlessons.com/episode147</u>
All about borshch — <u>ukrainianlessons.com/episode180</u>
Ukrainian cuisine in the Soviet times — <u>ukrainianlessons.com/episode181</u>
Local cuisines in Ukraine — <u>ukrainianlessons.com/episode182</u>
Modern gastronomy of Ukraine — <u>ukrainianlessons.com/episode183</u>
Coffee culture in Ukraine — <u>ukrainianlessons.com/episode184</u>

14. Clothing

 Link to audio: ukrainianlessons.com/ph-clothing

Do you need some clothing?	Вам потрібен одяг?	Vam potríben ódiah?
What clothes do you need?	Який одяг вам потрібен?	Yakýi ódiah vam potríben?
What size of clothes do you wear?	Який розмір одягу ви носите?	Yakýi rózmir ódiahu vy nósyte?
What size of clothes does your child wear?	Який розмір одягу носить ваша дитина?	Yakýi rózmir ódiahu nósyt vásha dytýna?
What is your shoe size?	Який у вас розмір взуття?	Yakýi u vas rózmir vzuttiá?
Do you need to buy new clothes?	Вам потрібно купити новий одяг?	Vam potríbno kupýty novýi ódiah?
I know a good shop.	Я знаю хороший магазин.	Ya znáiu khoróshyi mahazýn.
I know a good second hand shop.	Я знаю хороший секонд хенд.	Ya znáiu khoróshyi sékond khend.
Do you want to try it on?	Хочете це поміряти?	Khóchete tse pomíriaty?
Do you like it?	Вам подобається?	Vam podóbaietsia?
I like it.	Мені подобається.	Mení podóbaietsia.
It suits you.	Вам це личить.	Vam tse lýchyt.
How much does it cost?	Скільки це коштує?	Skílky tse kóshtuie?
This is cheap.	Це дешево.	Tse déshevo.
This is expensive.	Це дорого.	Tse dóroho.

Practice talking about **shopping for clothes and shoes** with these podcast episodes:
Shopping Vocabulary Booster — ukrainianlessons.com/fmu18
At the shoe shop — ukrainianlessons.com/episode31
Shopping for clothes — ukrainianlessons.com/episode32

clothes	одяг	ódiah
coat	пальто	paltó
dress	сукня	súknia
jacket	куртка	kúrtka
jeans	джинси	dzhýnsy
pajamas	піжама	pizháma
pants	штани	shtaný
raincoat	плащ	plashch
robe	халат	khalát
shirt	сорочка	soróchka
shorts	шорти	shórty
skirt	спідниця	spidnýtsia
socks	шкарпетки	shkarpétky
suit	костюм	kostiúm
sweater	светр	svetr
T-shirt	футболка	futbólka

underwear	спідня білизна	spídnia bilýzna
bra	бюстгальтер	biusthálter
panties, briefs, underpants	труси	trusý

shoes	взуття	vzuttiá
boots	черевики	cherevýky
sandals	сандалі	sandáli
slippers	капці	káptsi
sneakers	кросівки	krosívky

accessories	**аксесуари**	aksesuáry
belt	пояс	póias
cap	кепка	képka
comb	гребінець	hrebinéts
earrings	сережки	serézhky
glasses	окуляри	okuliáry
gloves	рукавички	rukavýchky
hat	шапка	shápka
jewelry	прикраси	prykrásy
mask	маска	máska
purse	сумочка	súmochka
ring	перстень	pérsten
scarf	шарф	sharf
sunglasses	сонцезахисні окуляри	sontsezakhysní okuliáry
umbrella	парасолька	parasólka
wallet	гаманець	hamanéts
watch	годинник	hodýnnyk

Watch this video to practice **clothing vocabulary with flashcards**:
ukrainianlessons.com/video-clothes

15. Money

Link to audio: **ukrainianlessons.com/ph-money**

This is for free.	Це безкоштовно.	Tse bezkoshtóvno.
I will pay for you.	Я заплачу за вас.	Ya zaplachú za vas.
Don't worry about the costs.	Не хвилюйтесь за витрати.	Ne khvyliúites za výtraty.
Do you have any money?	У вас є гроші?	U vas ye hróshi?
Do you have enough money?	У вас достатньо грошей?	U vas dostátno hróshei?
How much money do you have?	Скільки у вас є грошей?	Skílky u vas ye hróshei?
Do you know what cash benefits you are entitled to?	Чи знаєте ви, на які грошові виплати ви маєте право?	Chy znáiete vy, na yakí hroshoví výplaty vy máiete právo?
You can get a (one-time) cash benefit.	Ви можете отримати (одноразову) грошову допомогу.	Vy mózhete otrýmaty (odnorazóvu) hroshovú dopomóhu.
Can you access your bank account?	Ви маєте доступ до свого банківського рахунку?	Vy máiete dóstup do svohó bánkivskoho rakhúnku?
Do you have a valid credit/debit card?	У вас є робоча банківська картка?	U vas ye robócha bánkivska kártka?
Do you have any cash?	У вас є готівка?	U vas ye hotívka?
Do you need to withdraw some money?	Вам потрібно зняти гроші?	Vam potríbno zniáty hróshi?
Do you need help at the ATM?	Вам потрібна допомога з банкоматом?	Vam potríbna dopomóha z bankomátom?

| How much does it cost? | Скільки це коштує? | Skílky tse kóshtuie? |
| It costs... | Це коштує... | Tse kóshtuie... |

Find out more about **using numbers with currencies** on page 32.

You can pay...	**Ви можете заплатити...**	Vy mózhete zaplatýty...
by card (only)	(тільки) карткою	(tílky) kártkoiu
in cash (only)	(тільки) готівкою	(tílky) hotívkoiu

currencies	**валюта**	valiúta
hryvnia(s)	гривня (гривні)	hrývnia (hrývni)
dollar(s)	долар (долари)	dólar (dólary)
euro(s)	євро (євро)	yévro (yévro)
pound(s)	фунт (фунти)	funt (fúnty)
currency exchange	обмін валют	óbmin valiút

bank	**банк**	bank
I would like to open an account.	Я хочу відкрити рахунок.	Ya khóchu vidkrýty rakhúnok.
I would like to deposit some money in my account.	Я хочу покласти гроші на свій рахунок.	Ya khóchu poklásty hróshi na svii rakhúnok.
I would like to exchange currencies.	Я хочу обміняти валюту.	Ya khóchu obminiáty valiútu.
ATM	банкомат	bankomát

Listen to some **common conversations at the bank** in these podcast episodes:
Opening a bank account — ukrainianlessons.com/fmu6
At the bank in Ukraine — ukrainianlessons.com/episode84

16. Work & Employment

 Link to audio: ukrainianlessons.com/ph-work

work, job	робота	robóta
to work	працювати	pratsiuváty
I work full-time.	Я працюю на повний день.	Ya pratsiúiu na póvnyi den.
I work part-time.	Я працюю на неповний день.	Ya pratsiúiu na nepóvnyi den.
I work as a freelancer.	Я працюю на фрилансі.	Ya pratsiúiu na frylánsi.
I work from home.	Я працюю з дому.	Ya pratsiúiu z dómu.
I own a business.	У мене свій бізнес.	U méne svii bíznes.
I have a flexible schedule.	У мене гнучкий графік.	U méne hnuchkýi hráfik.
I work from Monday to Friday.	Я працюю з понеділка по п'ятницю.	Ya pratsiúiu z ponedílka po piátnytsiu.
I don't work.	Я не працюю.	Ya ne pratsiúiu.
Are you looking for a job?	Ви шукаєте роботу?	Vy shukáiete robótu?
Do you want to register as an unemployed person? (male / female)	Бажаєте зареєструватися як безробітний / безробітна?	Bazháiete zareiestruvátysia yak bezrobítnyi / bezrobítna?
Can I help you find a job?	Я можу допомогти вам знайти роботу?	Ya mózhu dopomohtý vam znaitý robótu?
What type of work are you looking for?	Який вид роботи ви шукаєте?	Yakýi vyd robóty vy shukáiete?

What can you do?	Що ви вмієте робити?	Shcho vy vmíiete robýty?
What was your job before?	Ким ви працювали раніше?	Kym vy pratsiuvály raníshe?
How long did you work at that job?	Як довго ви працювали на тій роботі?	Yak dóvho vy pratsiuvály na tii robóti?
What education do you have?	Яка у вас освіта?	Yaká u vas osvíta?
What are your salary expectations?	На яку зарплату ви розраховуєте?	Na yakú zarplátu vy rozrakhóvuiete?
Do you need help to prepare for the job interview?	Вам потрібна допомога з підготовкою до співбесіди?	Vam potríbna dopomóha z pidhotóvkoiu do spivbésidy?

days off	вихідні	vykhidní
education	освіта	osvíta
experience	досвід роботи	dósvid robóty
internship	стажування	stazhuvánnia
job interview	співбесіда	spivbésida
parental leave	декрет	dekrét
recommendations	рекомендації	rekomendátsii
resume	резюме	reziumé
salary	зарплата	zarpláta
sick leave	лікарняний	likarniányi
taxes	податки	podátky
unemployment office	бюро з працевлаштування	biuró z pratsevlashtuvánnia
vacancy	вакансія	vakánsiia
vacation	відпустка	vidpústka

professions (male / female) професії		profésii
actor	актор / акторка	aktór / aktórka
blogger	блогер / блогерка	blóher / blóherka
construction worker	будівельник / будівельниця	budivélnyk / budivélnytsia
dentist	стоматолог / стоматологиня	stomatóloh / stomatolohýnia
designer	дизайнер / дизайнерка	dyzáiner / dyzáinerka
developer	програміст / програмістка	prohramíst / prohramístka
doctor	лікар / лікарка	líkar / líkarka
driver	водій / водійка	vodíi / vodíika
engineer	інженер / інженерка	inzhenér / inzhenérka
journalist	журналіст / журналістка	zhurnalíst / zhurnalístka
lawer	юрист / юристка	yurýst / yurýstka
manager	менеджер / менеджерка	ménedzher / ménedzherka
nurse	медбрат / медсестра	medbrát / medsestrá
shop assistant	продавець / продавчиня	prodavéts / prodavchýnia
student	студент / студентка	studént / studéntka
teacher (at school)	вчитель / вчителька	vchýtel / vchýtelka
teacher (at university), instructor	викладач / викладачка	vykladách / vykladáchka
translator	перекладач / перекладачка	perekladách / perekladáchka
waiter	офіціант / офіціантка	ofitsiánt / ofitsiántka

Practice useful vocabulary for **jobs in Ukrainian** in these podcast episodes:
Male and female forms of professions — **ukrainianlessons.com/fmu34**
Jobs & professions vocabulary booster — **ukrainianlessons.com/fmu35**

17. Children

 Link to audio: ukrainianlessons.com/ph-children

child	**дитина**	dytýna
children	**діти**	díty
newborn	**новонароджена дитина**	novonaródzhena dytýna
baby	**немовля**	nemovliá
baby boy	**дівчинка**	dívchynka
baby girl	**хлопчик**	khlópchyk
toddler	**малюк, дитина**	maliúk, dytýna
teenager	**підліток**	pídlitok
parents	**батьки**	batký
mother	**мати**	máty
father	**батько**	bátko
legal guardian	**опікун**	opikún

Well done! Good kid!	**Молодець!**	Molodéts!
Don't be afraid.	**Не бійся.**	Ne bíisia.
Don't cry.	**Не плач.**	Ne plach.
Come here.	**Ходи сюди.**	Khodý siudý.
Everything is alright.	**Все добре.**	Vse dóbre.
Do you understand me?	**Ти розумієш мене?**	Ty rozumíiesh mené?
Do you need anything?	**Тобі щось потрібно?**	Tobí shchos potríbno?
Do you like it?	**Тобі подобається?**	Tobí podóbaietsia?
Do you need anything for the child?	**Вам потрібно щось для дитини?**	Vam potríbno shchos dlia dytýny?

Do you want to...?	Хочеш...?	Khóchesh...?
drink	пити	pýty
go to the toilet	в туалет	v tualét
pee	пісяти	písiaty
poo	какати	kákaty
play	гратися	hrátysia
sleep	спати	spáty
read a story	почитати казку	pochytáty kázku
call your mom	подзвонити мамі	podzvonýty mámi
listen to a song	послухати пісеньку	poslúkhaty písenku
watch a cartoon	подивитися мультик	podyvýtysia múltyk

Need to entertain Ukrainian kids? Play them one of these **Ukrainian cartoons**:
ukrainianlessons.com/ukrainian-cartoons

Please...	Будь ласка...	Bud láska...
sit down	сядь	siad
wash your hands	помий руки	pomýi rúky
try this	спробуй це	spróbui tse
put your clothes on	одягайся	odiaháisia
stop fooling around	припини дуріти	prypyný duríty
brush your teeth	почисть зуби	pochýst zúby

Let's go...	Ходімо...	Khodímo...
to eat	їсти	yísty
for a walk	гуляти	huliáty
outside	на вулицю	na vúlytsiu
to the playground	на дитячий майданчик	na dytiáchyi maidánchyk
to the kindergarten	в садочок	v sadóchok

Do you have...?	**У вас є...?**	U vas ye...?
Do you need...?	**Вам треба...?**	Vam tréba...?
Here is...	**Ось ...**	Os
baby bathtub	ванночка	vánnochka
baby bottle	пляшечка	pliáshechka
bib	слинявчик	slyniávchyk
blanket	ковдра	kóvdra
car seat	автокрісло	avtokríslo
changing table	пеленальний столик	pelenálnyi stólyk
crib	ліжечко	lízhechko
diaper	підгузок	pidhúzok
high chair	стільчик	stílchyk
pacifier	пустушка	pustúshka
potty	горщик	hórshchyk
stroller	візочок	vizóchok
towel	рушник	rushnýk
wet wipes	вологі серветки	volóhi servétky

feeding	**годування**	hoduvánnia
Do you breastfeed or bottle feed?	**Ви годуєте грудьми чи сумішшю?**	Vy hodúiete hrudmý chy súmishshiu?
Have you started on solids?	**Ви вже почали прикорм?**	Vy vzhe pochalý prykórm?
What does your child like to eat?	**Що ваша дитина любить їсти?**	Shcho vásha dytýna liúbyt yísty?
breast pump	**молоковідсмоктувач**	molokovidsmóktuvach
formula	**дитяча суміш**	dytiácha súmish
infant cereal	**дитяча каша**	dytiácha kásha

Do you want...?	Ви хочете...?	Vy khóchete...?
us to find you a babysitter?	щоб ми знайшли вам няню?	shchob my znaishlý vam niániu?
your baby to go to day care?	записати вашу дитину в яслі?	zapysáty váshu dytýnu v yásli?
your child to go to kindergarten here?	щоб ваша дитина ходила тут у садочок?	shchob vásha dytýna khodýla tut u sadóchok?
your child to go to school here?	щоб ваша дитина ходила тут у школу?	shchob vásha dytýna khodýla tut u shkólu?
toy	іграшка	íhrashka
toys	іграшки	íhrashky
ball	м'яч, м'ячик	miach, miáchyk
bicycle	велосипед	velosypéd
board game	настільна гра	nastílna hra
book (for kids)	книжечка	knýzhechka
car	машинка	mashýnka
coloring book	розмальовка	rozmalóvka
construction set	конструктор	konstrúktor
doll	лялька	liálka
jigsaw puzzle	пазл	pazl
markers	фломастери	flomástery
pencils	олівці	olivtsí
rattle	брязкальце	briázkaltse
roller skates	ролики	rólyky
scooter	самокат	samokát
stuffed animal	м'яка іграшка	miaká íhrashka
teether	гризунець	hryzunéts
toy blocks	кубики	kúbyky

18. Education

 Link to audio: **ukrainianlessons.com/ph-education**

school	школа	shkóla
elementary school	початкова школа	pochatkóva shkóla
middle school	середня школа	serédnia shkóla
high school	старша школа	stársha shkóla
public school	державна школа	derzhávna shkóla
private school	приватна школа	pryvátna shkóla
university	університет	universytét
student (at school) (male / female)	учень / учениця	úchen / uchenýtsia
student (at the university) (male / female)	студент / студентка	studént / studéntka
teacher (at school) (male / female)	вчитель / вчителька	vchýtel / vchýtelka
teacher (at the university) (male / female)	викладач / викладачка	vykladách / vykladáchka
principal (male / female)	директор / директорка	dyréktor / dyréktorka
classmate (male / female)	однокласник / однокласниця	odnoklásnyk / odnoklásnytsia
grade	клас	klas
first grade	перший клас	pérshyi klas
second grade	другий клас	drúhyi klas
third grade	третій клас	trétii klas

You can find a full list of ordinal numbers on page 35.

I am your teacher. (male / female)	Я ваш вчитель / Я ваша вчителька.	Ya vash vchýtel / Ya váshа vchýtelka.
Have you already enrolled your child in school?	Ви вже записали свою дитину до школи?	Vy vzhe zapysály svoiú dytýnu do shkóly?
Would you like to enroll your child in school?	Ви хочете записати вашу дитину до школи?	Vy khóchete zapysáty váshu dytýnu do shkóly?
Would you like to enroll your children in school?	Ви хочете записати ваших дітей до школи?	Vy khóchete zapysáty váshykh ditéi do shkóly?
What grade should he / she be in?	У якому класі він повинен / вона повинна бути?	U yakómu klási vin povýnen / voná povénna búty?

school subjects	**шкільні предмети**	shkilní predméty
Art	мистецтво	mystétstvo
Biology	біологія	biolóhiia
Chemistry	хімія	khímiia
Computer Science	інформатика	informátyka
English	англійська	anhlíiska
Geography	географія	heohráfiia
History	історія	istóriia
Foreign Languages	іноземні мови	inozémni móvy
Literature	література	literatúra
Mathematics	математика	matemátyka
Music	музика	múzyka
Physical Education	фізкультура	fizkultúra
Physics	фізика	fízyka

school supplies	**шкільне приладдя**	shkilné pryláddia
backpack	**рюкзак**	riukzák
book	**книга**	knýha
brush	**пензлик**	pénzlyk
calculator	**калькулятор**	kalkuliátor
colored pencils	**кольорові олівці**	koloróvi olivtsí
computer	**комп'ютер**	kompiúter
dictionary	**словник**	slovnýk
eraser	**гумка**	húmka
folder	**папка**	pápka
glue	**клей**	klei
laptop	**ноутбук**	noutbúk
map	**карта**	kárta
notebook	**зошит**	zóshyt
paints	**фарби**	fárby
paper	**папір**	papír
pen	**ручка**	rúchka
pencil	**олівець**	olivéts
pencil sharpener	**підстругачка**	pidstruháchka
ruler	**лінійка**	liníika
tablet	**планшет**	planshét
tape	**скотч**	skotch
textbook	**підручник**	pidrúchnyk

school life	шкільне життя	shkilné zhyttiá
board	дошка	dóshka
break	перерва	perérva
cafeteria	їдальня	yidálnia
classroom	класна кімната	klásna kimnáta
course	курс	kurs
curriculum	шкільна програма	shkilná prohráma
exam	екзамен	ekzámen
friend (male / female)	друг / подруга	druh / pódruha
friends	друзі	drúzi
grade (mark)	оцінка	otsínka
grades (marks)	оцінки	otsínky
homework assignments	домашнє завдання	domáshnie zavdánnia
library	бібліотека	bibliotéka
lunch	обід	obíd
playground	ігровий майданчик	ihrovýi maidánchyk
sandwich	бутерброд	buterbród
schedule of classes	розклад занять	rózklad zaniát
school bus	шкільний автобус	shkilnýi avtóbus
semester	семестр	seméstr
subject	предмет	predmét
summer vacation	літні канікули	lítni kaníkuly
test	тест, контрольна робота	test, kontrólna robóta

sport	**спорт**	sport
physical training	**фізкультура**	fizkultúra
warmup	**розминка**	rozmýnka
exercise	**зарядка**	zariádka
football	**футбол**	futból
basketball	**баскетбол**	basketból
volleyball	**волейбол**	voleiból
running	**біг**	bih
dance	**танці**	tántsi
ball	**м'яч**	miach
jump rope	**скакалка**	skakálka
sport uniform	**спортивна форма**	sportývna fórma
team	**команда**	kománda
competition	**змагання**	zmahánnia

Interested in learning **more about sports in Ukrainian**? Check out these
short podcast episodes:
Sports Vocabulary Booster – ukrainianlessons.com/fmu25
Talking about sport in Ukrainian – ukrainianlessons.com/fmu26

Curious to learn **more about education in Ukraine**? Then check out these podcast episodes:
Meeting the school's headmaster – ukrainianlessons.com/episode86
Teacher's Day in Ukraine – ukrainianlessons.com/episode87
University studies in Ukraine – ukrainianlessons.com/episode88
Postgraduate studies in Ukraine – ukrainianlessons.com/episode89
Education in Ukraine recap – ukrainianlessons.com/episode90
Higher education in Ukraine vs USA (in slow Ukrainian) – ukrainianlessons.com/episode189

19. Animals

 Link to audio: **ukrainianlessons.com/ph-animals**

animal, pet	**тварина**	tvarýna
animals, pets	**тварини**	tvarýny
dog	**собака**	sobáka
dogs	**собаки**	sobáky
cat	**кіт**	kit
cats	**коти**	kotý
breed	**порода**	poróda
mixed-breed	**безпородний**	bezporódnyi

What age is your dog / cat?	**Якого віку ваш собака / кіт?**	Yakóho víku vash sobáka / kit?
What breed is your dog / cat?	**Якої породи ваш собака / кіт?**	Yakói poródy vash sobáka / kit?
What is the name of your dog / cat?	**Як звати вашого собаку / кота?**	Yak zváty váshoho sobáku / kotá?
Does your pet have a microchip implant?	**Ваша тварина має мікрочіп?**	Vásha tvarýna máie míkrochip?
Is your dog / cat healthy?	**Ваш собака / кіт здоровий?**	Vash sobáka / kit zdoróvyi?
Is your animal sick of something?	**Ваша тварина на щось хворіє?**	Vásha tvarýna na shchos khvoríie?
Is your dog / cat vaccinated?	**Ваш собака / кіт вакцинований?**	Vash sobáka / kit vaktsynóvanyi?
Does your pet have a rabies vaccine?	**Ваша тварина має щеплення від сказу?**	Vásha tvarýna máie shchéplennia vid skázu?
Is your pet sterilized?	**Ваша тварина стерилізована?**	Vásha tvarýna sterylizóvana?

Your pet needs to see a veterinarian.	Вашій тварині потрібно до ветеринара.	Váshii tvarýni potríbno do veterynára.
Your pet needs treatment.	Вашій тварині потрібне лікування.	Váshii tvarýni potríbne likuvánnia.
Give pills once / twice a day.	Давайте таблетки один раз / два рази на день.	Daváite tablétky odýn raz / dva razý na den.
Has your pet been mistreated?	З вашою твариною поводилися жорстоко?	Z váshoiu tvarýnoiu povódylysia zhorstóko?
Please clean after your dog / cat.	Будь ласка, прибирайте після собаки / кота.	Bud láska, prybyráite píslia sobáky / kotá.
It's time to clean the cat's litter box.	Пора почистити котячий туалет.	Porá pochýstyty kotiáchyi tualét.
Does your pet have a veterinary certificate?	У вашої тварини є ветеринарний паспорт?	U váshoi tvarýny ye veterynárnyi pásport?
You can(not) go to this country with your pet.	Ви (не) можете їхати в цю країну з твариною.	Vy (ne) mózhete yíkhaty v tsiu kraínu z tvarýnoiu.

body parts	частини тіла	chastýny tíla
belly	живіт	zhyvít
ear	вухо	vúkho
ears	вуха	vukhá
muzzle	морда	mórda
paw	лапа	lápa
paws	лапи	lápy
tail	хвіст	khvist

Practice **talking about pets in Ukrainian** with this episode of Ukrainian Lessons Podcast:
My pets — ukrainianlessons.com/episode44

Learn **60+ words for animals in Ukrainian** with pictures & audio on this page:
Animals Vocabulary List — ukrainianlessons.com/animals-in-ukrainian-with-audio

20. War in Ukraine

 Link to audio: **ukrainianlessons.com/ph-war**

war	**війна**	viiná
martial law	**воєнний стан**	voiénnyi stan
military	**військовий**	viiskóvyi
army	**військо = армія**	víisko = ármiia
soldiers	**солдати**	soldáty
peace	**мир**	myr
UN	**ООН**	OÓN
NATO	**НАТО**	NÁTO
Ukraine	**Україна**	Ukraína
Armed Forces of Ukraine	**Збройні Сили України (ЗСУ)**	Zbróini Sýly Ukraíny (Ze e SU)
Territorial Defense	**Тероборона**	Teroboróna
Security Service of Ukraine	**Служба безпеки України**	Slúzhba bezpéky Ukraíny
President of Ukraine	**Президент України**	Prezydént Ukraíny
Volodymyr Zelenskyy	**Володимир Зеленський**	Volodýmyr Zelénskyi
Russia	**Росія**	Rosíia
enemy	**ворог**	vóroh
occupants	**окупанти**	okupánty
genocide	**геноцид**	henotsýd
dictator	**диктатор**	dyktátor
Vladimir Putin	**Володимир Путін**	Volodýmyr Pútin

weapon	**зброя**	zbróia
tank	**танк**	tank
artillery	**артилерія**	artylériia
drone	**дрон**	dron
missile	**ракета**	rakéta
shell	**снаряд**	snariád
shelling	**обстріли**	óbstrily
fighter jet	**винищувач**	vynýshchuvach
anti-tank weaponry	**протитанкова зброя**	protytánkova zbróia
air defense	**протиповітряна оборона (ППО)**	protypovítriana oboróna (PePeO)
bulletproof vest	**бронежилет**	bronezhylét
helmet	**шолом**	sholóm
nuclear weapon	**ядерна зброя**	yáderna zbróia

air raid sirens	**сирени повітряної тривоги**	syrény povítrianoi tryvóhy
Were there air raid sirens yesterday / nat night?	**Вчора / вночі були сирени?**	Vchóra / vnochí bulý syrény?
Did you hear air-raid sirens?	**Ви чули сирени?**	Vy chúly syrény?

| air raid shelter | **зброя** | ukryttiá |
| Is there an air raid shelter nearby? | **Поруч є укриття?** | Póruch ye ukryttiá? |

| curfew | **комендантська година** | komendántska hodýna |
| What is the curfew in your town? | **Яка комендантська година у вашому місті?** | Yaká komendántska hodýna u váshomu místi? |

donations	пожертвування	pozhértvuvannia
I want to help Ukraine financially.	Я хочу допомогти Україні фінансово.	Ya khóchu dopomohtý Ukraíni finánsovo.
I regularly transfer money to support Ukraine.	Я регулярно переказую гроші на підтримку України.	Ya rehuliárno perckázuiu hróshi na pidtrýmku Ukraíny.
How to donate money to the Ukrainian army?	Як пожертвувати гроші на українську армію?	Yak pozhértvuvaty hróshi na ukraínsku ármiiu?
How to donate money for humanitarian aid to Ukraine?	Як пожертвувати гроші на гуманітарну допомогу Україні?	Yak pozhértvuvaty hróshi na humanitárnu dopomóhu Ukraíni?
Do you know an organization in Ukraine that needs financial support?	Ви знаєте організацію в Україні, яка потребує фінансової підтримки?	Vy znáiete orhanizátsiiu v Ukraíni, yaká potrebúie finánsovoi pidtrýmky?

> If you wish to help Ukraine financially or in any other way,
> please check updated information at:
> ukrainianlessons.com/how-to-help-ukraine

national slogans	народні гасла	naródni hásla
Glory to Ukraine!	Слава Україні!	Sláva Ukraíni!
Glory to Heroes!	Героям Слава!	Heróiam Sláva!
Glory to the Armed Forces of Ukraine!	Слава ЗСУ!	Sláva Ze eS U!
Ukraine is in my heart.	Україна в моєму серці.	Ukraína v moiému sértsi.
Ukraine will win!	Україна переможе!	Ukraína peremózhe!
Everything will be Ukraine! (meaning Ukraine will win)	Все буде Україна!	Vse búde Ukraína!
"Life will win over death, and light will win over darkness" (Volodymyr Zelenskyy).	«Життя переможе смерть, а світло — темряву» (Володимир Зеленський).	Zhyttiá peremózhe smert, a svítlo — témriavu (Volodýmyr Zelénskyi).

About the Author

Anna Ohoiko is a Ukrainian language specialist, teacher, and founder of UkrainianLessons.com. She was born in 1991 – the year of birth of independent Ukraine. She is originally from the town of Polonne in Khmelnytska oblast, in central-western Ukraine. Having always been passionate about languages, Anna graduated from Kyiv-Mohyla Academy and got a Master's degree in Theory, History of Ukrainian Language and Comparative Studies.

After participating in the Revolution of Dignity in 2014, Anna decided to dedicate her professional life to popularizing the Ukrainian language internationally by teaching it in the most accessible and exciting way – through UkrainianLessons.com. In 2016, she started the Ukrainian Lessons Podcast, which she designed as a step-by-step Ukrainian audio course for beginners. Since then, it has grown into a comprehensive language program for all levels.

From 2017 to 2018, she taught Ukrainian at the University of Pennsylvania through the Fulbright program. As of 2022, she works from her home office in Sweden, bringing inspiring resources for learning Ukrainian out there to the world.

Anna is clearly a brilliant linguist and manages to convey masses of information in an engaging and exciting way. It means a lot that she has created a resource that is so helpful and accessible for Ukrainian language learners and that includes contemporary Ukrainian culture.

Irene SanPietro from NYC

Anna is an amazing teacher! It's so obvious that she is indeed a trained teacher who knows how to convey information so that it is retained well.

Amy McCoy from North Carolina

I decided to listen to one or two podcasts for interest's sake, but when Anna speaks on podcasts, it's as if she's there in person to teach you.

Shavonn Kravets from New Holland, PA

Anna is so charming and engaging, and her lessons are a delightful incentive to revive dormant vocabulary and traditions. Dedicated to the last syllable and motivating. It's always a pleasure to listen to her charming голосочок. Анна фантастична and for anyone seriously interested in learning Ukrainian, her podcast is the place to be.

Rahneda Breker from the United States

Anna's sense of humor and her love of her culture comes through in the podcasts and makes the learning experience fun. Even though I don't usually eat beets, I am now eager to try the red borscht!

Mary Margaret Perez from Watsonville, California

About Ukrainian Lessons

This phrasebook was brought to you by UkrainianLessons. com — a cozy educational platform that provides good quality modern materials for learning Ukrainian. It was created by Anna Ohoiko shortly after the Ukrainian Revolution of Dignity in 2014. Since then, the UL team has been providing various materials and support for Ukrainian learners with blog posts, books, videos, infographics, and their structured podcast courses — Ukrainian Lessons Podcast and 5 Minute Ukrainian.

We are also proud to host the most active Ukrainian learners community on Facebook — a group where everyone can ask questions, practice Ukrainian and share their favorite materials. You can join this friendly community at **ukrainianlessons.com/fbgroup**.

I am so happy to have stumbled upon this site/podcast! It is wonderful that the Ukrainian Lessons Podcast is working to address that inaccessibility by providing the free podcast & an abundance of resources to further our language and cultural learning.

Lilly F from the United States

I think the Ukrainian language is the most beautiful of all the Slavic languages due to its musicality and rhythm... I feel lucky to come across Anna's way of teaching it! It is friendly and very well focused on securing the steps one by one as I am progressing through the entire course. And the best part is that it doesn't stop at the basics... It gets gradually more difficult as you go... Lovely! I would recommend everyone to subscribe to the premium membership. It justifies its value 100%... better when you leave your українські friends amazed by your progress in their beautiful language.

Luis A. Zapata from Peru

On my first visit to Kyiv, I felt confident in my already obtained basic skills in Ukrainian and was even slightly complimented in a souvenir shop. I owe a good deal a huge credit to ukrainianlessons.com and Anna. She takes you into this language, gradually enhancing new words and grammar.

Wilhelm Fuchs from Germany

You can find it all here in a most palatable and well-prepared mix — grammar, vocabulary, pronunciation, language functions — all served up engagingly with a serving of cultural knowledge topping it up like a spoonful of сметана! It doesn't get any better than this!

Христина Сікорська from Winnipeg, Canada

More from Ukrainian Lessons

Ukrainian Lessons Podcast

Are you looking for a well structured and easily accessible Ukrainian language course that can easily fit into your life? Ukrainian Lessons Podcast is exactly what its name says: Lessons of Ukrainian in the format of a podcast. This means you can enjoy learning Ukrainian with a real teacher from the comfort of your car, on your morning jog, or while cooking. Give it a go — all the lessons are free — and if you enjoy it and want to dig deeper, subscribe to the premium membership to receive PDF lesson notes and digital flashcards.

Find out more at **ukrainianlessons.com/thepodcast** or look for Ukrainian Lessons Podcast in your podcast app.

5 Minute Ukrainian

This series of mini-lessons is all about conversations. Each episode of 5 Minute Ukrainian contains a short dialogue that you will listen to at a natural and slow speed. Then your host Anna will teach you some essential phrases for that particular situation. Apart from the dialogues, there are also useful vocabulary boosters and grammar point episodes. You can also subscribe to receive comprehensive lesson notes with exercises and flashcards.

Find out more at **ukrainianlessons.com/fmu** or look for 5 Minute Ukrainian in your podcast app.

1000 Most Useful Ukrainian Words Book

If you are looking for a huge vocabulary boost at the beginning of your Ukrainian learning journey, check out this resource. It provides you with 1000 Ukrainian words and examples of using them in simple sentences — all with English translations. There is also a set of digital flashcards that can be used with the Anki app to learn these words quicker with audio and pictures.

Find out more at **ukrainianlessons.com/1000words**

Easy Ukrainian Book (intermediate & advanced level)

If you already have some progress in Ukrainian and looking for an immersive experience, check out this book. It is an easy read with exercises, vocabulary lists, and audio. Its fun story is about Beatrice from Spain and Brian from the USA who are going to have an unforgettable summer in Ukraine... Available as paperback or ebook — whichever format you choose, you get free audio!

Find out more at **ukrainianlessons.com/cossack**

Made in the USA
Coppell, TX
02 January 2023

10232361R00058